# The Unofficial Alabama Trivia, Puzzles & History Book

Dale Ratermann



BLUE RIVER PRESS

Blue River Press
Indianapolis, Indiana

*The Unofficial Alabama Trivia, Puzzles & History Book*


ISBN-13: 9781935628125

Cover Design: Phil Velikan
Cover Photo: Russell Grace (www.RussellGraceImages.com)
Illustrations: Robert Jackson
Layout: MaryKay Hruskocy Scott
Proofread by: MaryKay Hruskocy Scott

Printed in the United States of America
10 9 8 7 6 5 4 3 2 1

Blue River Press
Distributed by Cardinal Publishers Group
Tom Doherty Company, Inc.
www.cardinalpub.com

## Table of Contents

## Short Yardage Crossword

Solution on page 133.

**Across**

1. Tide DE from 1988-91 from Holt, Ala., Steve ___
5. UA fraternity letter
8. Do-___ (extra tries)
10. Bama crew need
11. Home country of UA track star David Kimani
12. Genetic stuff
13. Impaled
15. Pro hoops league
16. Holds back
20. J.D. Byrider product
21. Sneaker sole pattern
23. Football air pressure meas.
24. Christmas decoration
25. Had a pizza at Mellow Mushroom
26. Tide shoe sponsor

**Down**

1. Hokkaido restaurant pan
2. Nights before big games
3. Crooked
4. "Bear"
5. The C in UPC
6. UA DE who played nine seasons for the Colts (1986-94)
7. Bank of Tuscaloosa offering
9. Holy day
14. UA All-American safety in 2010, Mark ___
16. UA All-American in 1941 who was elected to the Alabama House of Representatives
17. One of the Great Lakes
18. Schlotzsky's, e.g.
19. Polio vaccine developer
20. Bama bean counter, for short
22. Turn crimson, perhaps

After solving the crossword puzzle, use the letters in the grid to answer this additional clue. Transfer the letters in numbered boxes to the corresponding blanks below. (Or answer the additional clue first to help you solve the crossword puzzle.)

All-American receiver (1966) who also coached the Tide (1987-90)

___ ___ ___ ___ ___ ___ ___

23 2 16 11 7 26 9

## Chapter 1

# History

The University of Alabama's first football team began playing in 1892. Since then, the Crimson Tide has become one of the most successful and most supported squads in the country. Alabama lays claim to 13 national championships and 26 conference titles. In addition, the school has participated in 58 bowl games.

The football team was started by a UA law student, William G. Little, who had learned the game while attending school in Massachusetts. Little was the captain of the 19-man squad; E.B. Beaumont was the head coach.

UA's first game was against a team made up of Birmingham high school players. The game was played on a baseball field in Birmingham, and UA won, 56-0. That first team included William B. Bankhead, who became the Speaker of the U.S. House of Representatives, and Bibb Graves, who became the Governor of Alabama. The next day, UA played a team representing the Birmingham Athletic Club, and lost, 5-4. Bama won a rematch with the Birmingham A.C. a month later (14-0), then played Auburn in Birmingham later in the school year. Auburn won that first match-up between state schools, 32-22.

The following season, Eli Abbott took over the coaching reins, and UA finished 0-4. In 1894, Bama went 3-1, including an 18-0 win over Auburn. In 1896, the University trustees passed a rule that forbid school teams from traveling off campus. So, only one game was played in 1897, and the football team was disbanded in 1898.

The team resumed play in 1899, but it wasn't until 1922 that Bama first gained national recognition. That was when UA beat Penn, 9-7, in Philadelphia. Wallace Wade was named the team's coach a year later, and in 1925 he led Alabama to a 10-0 record, a win in the Rose Bowl over Washington and the school's first national championship. Wade's teams were undefeated and national champions again in 1926 and '30.

Frank Thomas took over as head coach in 1931 and led Alabama to two national titles (1934 and '41) and an undefeated season in 1945. After Harold Drew's teams went 54-28-7 from 1947-54, he was replaced by J.B. Whitworth. In three seasons, Whitworth's teams were just 4-24-2, including a 14-game losing streak. Following successive 2-7-1 seasons, Whitworth was fired and Bear Bryant was hired.

In Bryant's first season (1958), the Tide went 5-4-1. In his fourth season, they won the national championship, the first of six under Bryant's leadership.

But Bryant's 25 years as head coach included some controversial moments as well. The University admitted its first African-American student in 1956. The first sustained enrollment of African-Americans was in 1963. But the football team remained all white until the Tide was soundly beaten by Southern Cal and its African-American stars in the 1970 Rose Bowl.

That's when UA opened the door to African-American players. Running back Wilbur Jackson was the first African-American player offered a football scholarship; junior college transfer John Mitchell was the first African-American player to start. Alabama improved to 11-1 in 1971, went 10-2 in '72, then won another national championship in 1973. UA added back-to-back national titles (1978 and '79) before Bryant retired following the 1982 season.

Gene Stallings returned the Tide to prominence with a 13-0 record and national championship in 1992. Nick Saban continued the success in 2009 with a 14-0 record and BCS Championship Game victory. That was also the year Alabama had its first Heisman Trophy winner, Mark Ingram, Jr.

## Who Am I? Sudoku

Use logic to fill in the boxes so every row, column and 3x3 box contains the letters in the name of a memorable Alabama player. (Hint: He was a defensive standout who led the 1986 team in fumble recoveries.) When completed, the row indicated by the arrow will spell out his name correctly. Solution on page 133.

| | | | | | | | | | |
|---|---|---|---|---|---|---|---|---|---|
| | | | E | | T | L | G | | |
| | L | A | | | | S | | | |
| | H | | | G | | | A | | |
| | | | R | T | | | | H | G |
| ► | | | | | | | | | |
| | G | H | | | | E | L | | |
| | | | U | | | T | | | S |
| | | | | E | | | | U | T |
| | | | H | L | U | | E | | |

## Ingram Sudoku

Use logic to fill in the boxes so every row, column and 2x3 box contains the letters I-N-G-R-A-M, in honor of Mark Ingram, the only Alabama player to win the Heisman Trophy. Solution on page 133.

| | | | | | |
|---|---|---|---|---|---|
| | | G | | | R |
| | | N | | A | |
| G | | | N | | M |
| N | | I | | | A |
| | N | | A | | |
| I | | | R | | |

## Bama Hodgepodge

Find items in the categories listed, going up, down, sideways or diagonally in the letter grid. No letter is used more than once. When you have found all 21 items, there will be 56 unused letters. Starting at the top of the grid, moving from left to right, and working down, fill in the spaces below the grid with those unused letters to spell out a hidden phrase. Hint: The phrase is part of a Bama fight song. (Bonus points if you know the song's title.) Solution on page 134.

**6 UA Football All-Americans**

______________________

______________________

______________________

______________________

______________________

______________________

**5 Former UA Coaches**

______________________

______________________

______________________

______________________

______________________

**4 UA Bowl Games**

______________________

______________________

______________________

______________________

**3 SEC Rivals**

______________________

______________________

______________________

**2 UA Colors**

______________________

______________________

**1 UA Athletics Director**

______________________

Y

E A A

W H I T E

S B R Y A N T

P N L O W E C E L

C E O A B R A S O R M

A O R Y D O R O M Y O O C

W D K L S N B O A N E K R

M Y I E T U O N I U D E I

E V N E D R S R Y S B A M

N M S A E M A N S B E H S

S R I N D Y O U H I T Y O

S U U T E N N E S S E E N

H G B O U G U R S H S

U A U T A S R A A

L R A T L N B

A I O D A

D R N

E

**Hidden Phrase:**

___ ___ ___, ___ ___ ___ ___ ___ ___ ___!

___ ___ ___ ___ ___ '___ ___ ___ ___ ___ ___!

___ ___ ___ ___ ___ '___ ___ ___ ___ ___ ___ ___'___

___ ___ ___ ___ ___ ___ ___ ___ ___; ___ ___ ___

___ ___ ___ ___ ___ ___ ___ ___ ___ ___!

## History Crossword

Solution on page 134.

**Across**

1. 1968 All-American LB from Tarrant, Ala.
5. 1996 All-American LB from Batesville, Miss.
9. 1,000+ yards rusher in 2004 and '05
14. Black and white cookie at Winn-Dixie
15. UA computer operator
16. Be crazy about Bama
17. Player's backside
18. Toothpaste holder
19. Campus think tank nuggets
20. Exposed, like a campus streaker
22. Freely (2 wds.)
24. Common UA soccer score
26. Sisters' daughters
30. 1962 All-American C/LB from Excel, Ala.
34. Locks at Bear Creek Stables
36. Sound at Belle La Vie Spa
37. Opera Birmingham solo
38. Birmingham Race Course hoof sound
40. Char at Longhorn Steakhouse
42. New ___ Baptist Church
43. The Capstone, e.g.
45. Alabama Dermatology concern
46. Some sorority women
48. Like a player's Hummer
49. Spirits Inc. beverages
50. Tuscaloosa-to-Atlanta dir.
51. Tuscaloosa County Court jury member
53. 1964 All-American QB from Beaver Falls, Pa.
55. 15th ___ Diner
57. Pittsburgh Pirates stadium name
58. Stir up a rowdy crowd
61. Ham it up for The ACT
66. Pregame coin toss choice
69. Spirited horse
71. Sailor's cry
72. Rajah's wife
73. A ___ pittance
74. Tick off the refs
75. UA QB who was a two-time Super Bowl MVP
76. Leading receiver in 1985 and '86
77. UA starting QB in 1974 and '75

**Down**

1. Game ender, perhaps
2. 205: UA's ___ code
3. Stadium restroom plumbing problem
4. Old stories of Bama football
5. Same old, same old
6. Mugshots Bar order, with "the"
7. Money owed to Bryant Bank
8. Sketched in a UA art class
9. Like *The Tuscaloosa News* and *Birmingham News*
10. Befuddle
11. Eggs at Wintzell's Oyster House
12. Victoria's Secret item
13. "Absolutely!"
21. Genetic stuff
23. Jameson ___
25. 1/36th of a yard
27. Kind of cooking oil
28. Young raptor at Guntersville State Park
29. "Good grief!"

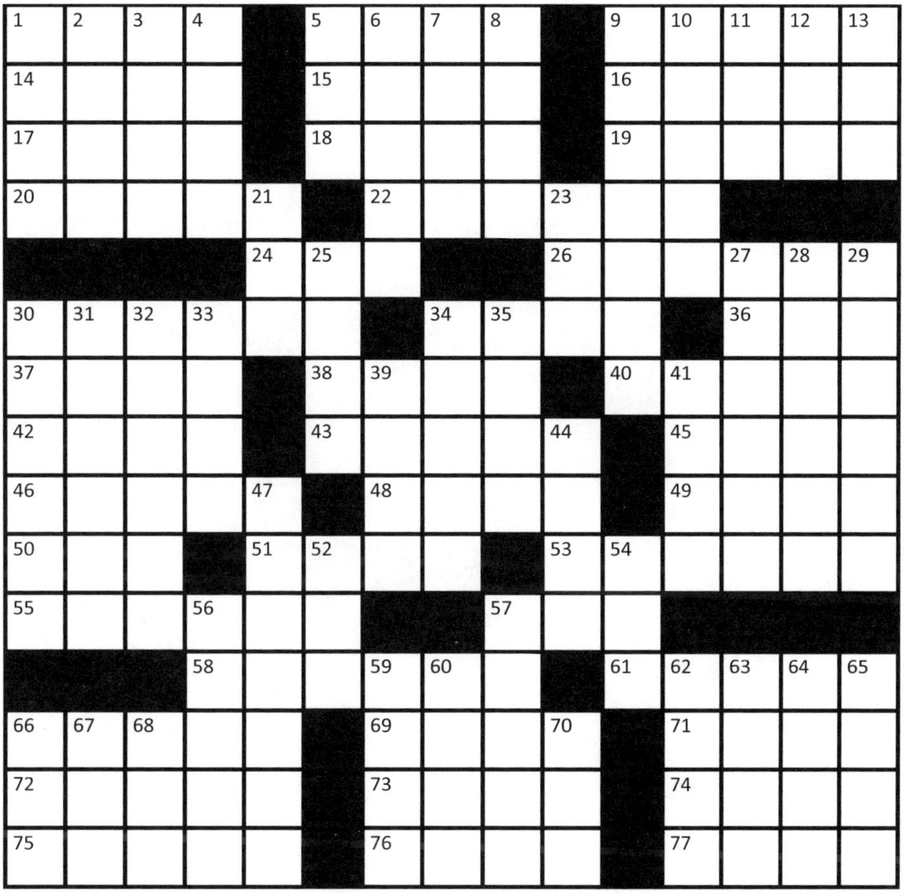

30. Spiffs (up)
31. *Murder on the ___ Express*
32. Out of control BCS championship postgame reveler
33. UA gymnastics All-American, ___ Duckworth
34. Part of Alabama DMV
35. Cheaha Mountain, in Alabama
39. Earring site
41. Islamic Society of Tuscaloosa prayer leader
44. Super Bowl X MVP, ___ Swann
47. ___*: For Hire* (Robert Urich TV series)
52. Catchall abbr.
54. Hole-in-one at the UA Golf Course
56. Downy duck
57. Gem strung at Hudson-Poole Jewelers
59. Slash Pine Poetry Festival foot
60. Geneva State Forest unit
62. K or Wal follower
63. A Buckeye's home state
64. Tattled
65. Gawked at the cheerleaders
66. Mins. and mins.
67. Have the shrimp & grits at Evangeline's
68. Start of a Tide cheer: "Gimme ___!" (2 wds.)
70. ___-Aire Motel

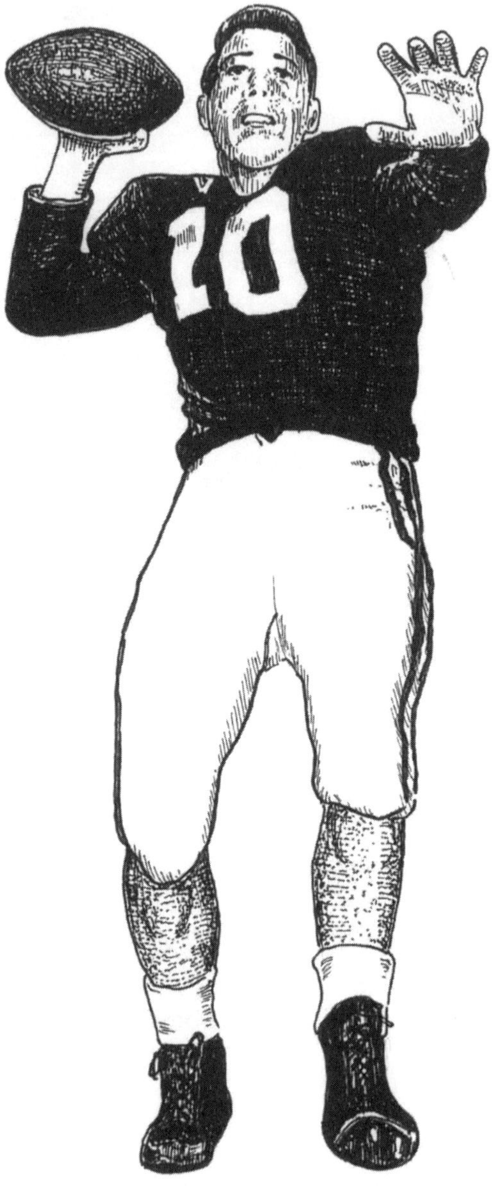

*Bart Starr*

## History Trivia

Answers on page 135.

1. Who are the only two Bama players who were chosen to the All-America team three times?

2. Which defensive back caused UA to forfeit eight games and one tie in the 1993 season because he secretly signed with an agent prior to the season?

3. What is the school record for consecutive victories set from 1978-80 and matched from 1991-93?

4. The Tide's first win over a team ranked No. 1 in the country was in 1977. Which school did UA beat?

5. What year did Alabama crack the final Top 10 AP poll for the first time?

6. When did Bama move to No. 1 in the AP poll for the first time?

7. Bear Bryant was the UA coach for 25 years. What was Bama's record in his 25 Homecoming games?

8. Alabama is first in the All-Time SEC standings. Who is second?

9. The Tide made a significant change to their game jerseys in 1981. What was different that year?

10. Name the four UA head coaches in the College Football Hall of Fame.

11. Which school did Alabama beat in the Independence Bowl in Nick Saban's first season at UA?

12. Which two Bama players have won the Butkus Award, given to the nation's top linebacker?

13. Name the three Tide quarterbacks in the College Football Hall of Fame.

14. Who are the four players who played at UA in the 1970s who are in the College Football Hall of Fame?

15. According to *bleacherreport.com*, who was the greatest of "The 50 Greatest Players in Crimson Tide History"?

16. What is the name of Bama's elephant mascot?

17. Does Bryant-Denny Stadium have a playing surface made of grass or artificial turf?

18. When was the last Alabama football game at Legion Field?

19. Recite the Rammer Jammer Cheer.

20. Now sing the chorus of *Alma Mater*.

21. What is the official capacity of Bryant-Denny Stadium?

22. Who won MVP awards at the Bluebonnet Bowl as a sophomore (in a tie with Texas) and the Orange Bowl as a senior (in a win over Oklahoma)?

23. Which Bama All-American quarterback threw a 52-yard touchdown pass on the first play of his college career?

24. Which UA receiver finished his four-year career with an SEC record of 20.3 yards per catch?

25. Match these nicknames with the Alabama All-Americans:

| | |
|---|---|
| Cisco | Millard Howell |
| Dixie | Vaughn Mancha |
| General | Johnny Musso |
| The Italian Stallion | Riley Smith |

## Short Yardage Crossword

Solution on page 136.

**Across**

1. Norm at the UA Golf Course
4. CB on Tide's 1992 national championship team, ___ Shade
7. Genetic stuff
8. PC "brain"
9. Regular season football mo.
10. Spring football mo.
11. Ultimate degree
12. All-American QB on Tide's 1965 national championship team
14. Short-lived TV show, ___ *Love*
16. All-American DE on Tide's 1992 national championship team
17. ___-tac-toe
18. Calendar square
19. "___ boom bah!"
20. UA psych class topic
21. Fresh from the oven at Hungry Howie's
22. Richard Shelby pos.
23. Hannah pair?

**Down**

1. Sticks out
2. Alaskan port
3. Terminix target
4. It's stepped on in the locker room
5. Allocate
6. Campus wall painters
11. WVTM network affiliation
12. Withdrawn
13. Loc. of the Heisman Trophy Awards Dinner
15. Check for fit at Aeropostale (2 wds.)
19. Cow or sow at the Alabama State Fair

After solving the crossword puzzle, use the letters in the grid to answer this additional clue. Transfer the letters in numbered boxes to the corresponding blanks below. (Or answer the additional clue first to help you solve the crossword puzzle.)

All-American DB on 2009 national championship team who also returned punts

___ ___ ___ ___ ___ ___
5 3 20 11 10 19

## Chapter 2

# Championship Teams

The 2009 Alabama football season began with high expectations. After all, the 2008 team was 12-0 and ranked No. 1 in the nation entering the SEC Championship Game. A loss to No. 2 Florida in that game, followed by a loss to No. 7 Utah in the Sugar Bowl, put a damper on that season, but inspired the returning players (including 16 starters) to work even harder in the 2009 campaign.

But the 2009 team would have a new starting quarterback (Greg McElroy) and a new starting running back (Mark Ingram). To top it off, based on the previous season's performances, Alabama's 2009 schedule was rated the toughest of the 120 Division I FBS teams. Bama opened the season ranked No. 5 in the country. They faced the nation's No. 7 ranked team, Virginia Tech, in the season opener. Bama scored 18 fourth quarter points en route to a 34-24 come-from-behind win.

McElroy continued to improve as the season progressed, Ingram piled up rushing yards, and the defensive unit was one of the best in the nation. Bama knocked off Florida International, North Texas, Arkansas and Kentucky, before trouncing No. 20 Ole Miss, 22-3. Following a 20-6 win over No. 22 South Carolina, the 7-0 Tide moved to No. 1 in the rankings. That set up a showdown with Tennessee. The Tide held on for a 12-10 win behind four field goals from Leigh Tiffin. The Tide blocked Tennessee's 45-yard field goal attempt on the final play of the game.

The close call dropped the Tide to No. 3 in the polls, but they cruised past No. 9 LSU, Mississippi State and Tennessee-Chattanooga prior to the annual Iron Bowl game at Auburn. Bama scored the go-ahead touchdown with 1:24 to play (a four-yard pass from McElroy to third-string tailback Roy Upchurch) and held on for a 26-21 win.

That set the stage for the SEC Championship Game between No. 1 Florida and No. 2 Alabama. The Tide took the lead, 3-0, on their initial possession and never trailed on their way to a 32-13 win.

No. 1 Alabama was in the BCS Championship Game against No. 2 Texas. The Longhorns' All-America quarterback, Colt McCoy, was knocked out of the game early, but Texas still held a 6-0 lead heading into the second quarter. Ingram scored a touchdown from two yards out to give Bama the lead, and they held on for a 37-21 victory.

After the season, a statue of Saban was erected on the Walk of Champions outside of Bryant-Denny Stadium. "The statue is going to represent what that team accomplished," Saban said. "Their names are all going to be on the national championship plaque."

That was the most recent of 13 national championships and 26 conference titles, including 22 SEC championships. But what constitutes a "national championship"? According to the NCAA football records book, "During the last 138 years, there have been more than 30 selectors of national champions using polls, historical research and mathematical rating systems. Beginning in 1936, the Associated Press began the best-known and most widely circulated poll of sportswriters and broadcasters. Before 1936, national champions were determined by historical research and retroactive ratings and polls . . . the criteria for being included in this historical list of poll selectors is that the poll be national in scope, either through distribution in newspaper, television, radio and/or computer online."

In addition to the 13 championships claimed by UA, the NCAA recognizes four other Alabama teams that were No. 1 in at least one final poll: 1945 (10-0), 1966 (11-0), 1975 (11-1) and 1977 (11-1). That brings UA's total to 17, by the NCAA's count.

## Neighbors Sudoku

Use logic to fill in the boxes so every row, column and 3x3 box contains the letters N-E-I-G-H-B-O-R-S, in honor of Billy Neighbors. The two-way player on the 1961 national championship team is a member of the College Football Hall of Fame. Solution on page 137.

| | | | | | | | | |
|---|---|---|---|---|---|---|---|---|
| R | | | | N | | | | S |
| | | | | | | | | |
| | | S | G | | O | E | | |
| | | N | H | | B | S | | |
| I | | | | | | | | R |
| | | E | S | | G | H | | |
| | | O | R | | H | B | | |
| | | | | | | | | |
| N | | | | E | | | | G |

## Jordan Sudoku

Use logic to fill in the grid so every row, column and 2x3 box contains the letters J-O-R-D-A-N, in honor of Lee Roy Jordan. The All-American linebacker helped the Crimson Tide win the 1961 national championship. Solution on page 136.

| | | | | | |
|---|---|---|---|---|---|
| | | D | | | |
| | R | A | J | | |
| | | R | O | N | |
| | N | J | A | | |
| | | O | R | A | |
| | | | D | | |

## Championship Teams Word Search

Find these 36 members of Alabama's 2009 national championship team. The names run up, down, forward, backward and diagonally. Solution on page 136.

| | | | | | | | | | | | | | | |
|---|---|---|---|---|---|---|---|---|---|---|---|---|---|---|
| G | Y | Q | R | E | B | U | H | B | A | R | R | O | N | R |
| H | V | V | I | Z | F | L | N | O | S | N | H | O | J | O |
| M | A | R | G | N | I | A | L | C | C | M | T | Y | P | G |
| N | I | F | F | I | T | I | Z | A | T | G | M | A | Z | E |
| S | N | K | Y | Y | Z | D | R | G | N | I | K | J | N | R |
| I | O | U | C | J | G | P | W | I | L | L | I | A | M | S |
| V | M | H | O | I | E | W | H | C | R | U | H | C | P | U |
| A | C | N | C | N | R | S | A | N | E | R | A | K | R | E |
| D | E | T | T | A | A | E | H | H | A | N | K | S | E | R |
| S | L | E | Z | W | L | C | D | A | S | N | C | O | A | A |
| G | R | E | E | N | D | V | T | A | R | P | D | N | M | D |
| C | O | H | I | G | H | T | O | W | E | R | U | E | E | P |
| O | Y | L | L | A | D | O | O | W | E | D | I | K | R | K |
| D | Y | H | V | M | C | C | O | Y | E | L | L | E | M | S |
| Y | K | E | E | P | P | C | J | O | R | D | A | N | F | H |

| | | | |
|---|---|---|---|
| ANDERS | FITZGERALD | JORDAN | SHARRIEF |
| ARENAS | GREEN | KING | SMELLEY |
| BARRON | HANKS | MAZE | TIFFIN |
| CARPENTER | HIGHTOWER | MCCLAIN | UPCHURCH |
| CODY | HUBER | MCCOY | UPSHAW |
| DAREUS | INGRAM | MCELROY | VLACHOS |
| DAVIS | JACKSON | PEEK | WASHINGTON |
| DEADERICK | JOHNSON | REAMER | WILLIAMS |
| DIAL | JONES | ROGERS | WOODALL |

## Word Builder

Using just the nine letters in the grid, find the answers to each clue. Every answer must include the highlighted letter E. Answers on page 135.

| | | |
|---|---|---|
| B | K | A |
| R | **E** | J |
| A | Y | R |

**3 Letters**

1. Helmet hole site
2. Off week in the schedule
3. Stadium lock opener
4. Confederate flag flyer
5. Jason's Deli bread

**4 Letters**

6. UA geometry class calculation
7. Sophomore, e.g.
8. Coach Bryant moniker
9. Like a 60-yard field goal

**5 Letters**

10. Smoothie King fruit
11. Gas pedal neighbor
12. University gardener, at times

**6 Letters**

13. Jack Hamm's sweet shop

**9 Letters**

14. QB on 1992 national championship team (2 wds.)

## Championship Teams Crossword

Solution on page 138.

**Across**

1. Manufacture
5. 1992 national title team TE, ___ Mangum
9. Full of chutzpah, like a Blue Chip recruit
14. Fairy tale villain
15. Campus map notation: You Are ___
16. Rodeo performer
17. Not imagined
18. CVS hand lotion ingredient
19. Tall tales about Bama's "good ol' days"
20. Birmingham Zoo wildebeests
21. 1966 national title team QB, ___ Stabler
22. Large amount of money from Regions Bank
23. *The Tuscaloosa News* revenue source
24. Kind of Alabama tax
25. Came out ahead in the game
26. UA fraternity letter
29. Twangy, as a voice
31. Fortuneteller's card
33. Buchanan Custom Homes site
34. Expected
36. UGA color
37. Memorial Day solo
38. Chapter heading and puzzle theme
42. Proper's partner
43. Doctrine: Suffix
44. "Are we there ___?"
45. Gun, as a NASCAR engine
46. Trojan War epic
48. Alabama Guard helicopter part
52. Be in the red
53. Some Tuscaloosa City Council votes
54. ET's craft
56. Opp. of WSW
57. IHOP omelet ingredient
58. Tera Lane, e.g.
59. Timbuktu's land
60. Kind of energy
63. Indonesian vacation island
64. Opposin', in the Alabama hills
65. La Scala offering
66. Declare
67. Player's iPod selection
68. Sacred hymn
69. Like many a head-turner on campus
70. Pay attention to

**Down**

1. 1966 national title team FB, Ed ___
2. To-do list for Nick Saban
3. 1978 national title team LB, Barry ___
4. Bento sushi fish
5. Uniform shade?
6. Give in to a player's demands
7. It's pumped in the team's weight room
8. Understand
9. 6-time national title team coach
10. Tuscaloosa's Culver or Hargrove, e.g.
11. Football spring practice mo.
12. Jeff Sessions' pos.
13. Redbox rental: *48* ___
22. Resembling the Tuskegee National Forest
24. Auburn urban renewal target

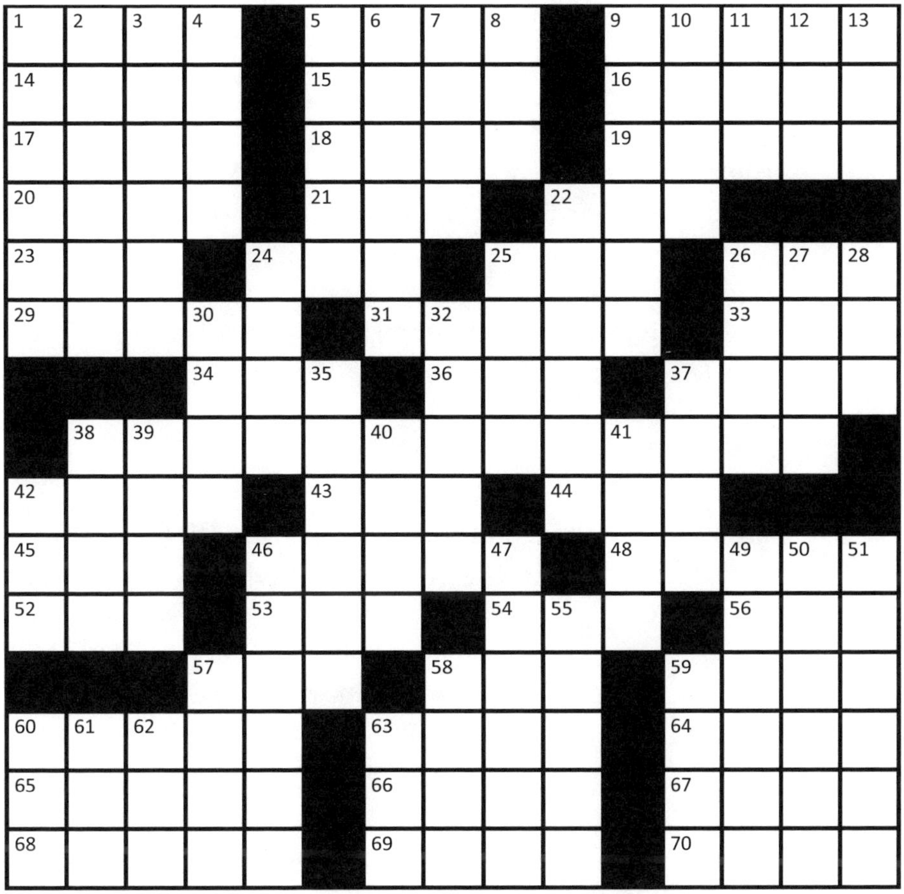

25. Small Alabama songbird
26. Applaud for a Tide TD
27. Back Forty Beer Company needs
28. Part of TGIF
30. 1999 SEC title team TB/LB, ___ Cox
32. Jack Hamm's Bakery emanation
35. Final words of a UA textbook
37. 1998 Bama LB, ___ Smith
38. UA sport with oars
39. Georgia Tech center of activity?
40. Egyptian goddess
41. Jason's Deli sandwich
42. Paid football player, briefly
46. 2009 national title team RB, Mark ___
47. Two-unit home on campus
49. 1992 national title team CB, George ___
50. Surfing in one's dorm room
51. Restrained, as a horse
55. Tinkerbell, for one
57. 1981 SEC title team FB, ___ Collins
58. UA relief pitcher's stat
59. College trig or calc
60. Soak (up)
61. Player photo ___ (camera sessions)
62. Grazing area
63. Some UA degrees

## Championship Teams Trivia

Answers on page 137.

1. Which Bama wide receiver ran 77 yards for a touchdown after lining up as the quarterback in the 1999 SEC Championship Game win over Florida?

2. In the 2010 BCS Championship Game, who knocked Texas QB Colt McCoy out of the game in the first quarter with his big hit?

3. In that same game, who intercepted Texas QB Garrett Gilbert's final pass attempt to seal the win?

4. Which school did UA beat in the inaugural SEC Championship Game in 1992?

5. Which school did UA beat in the Sugar Bowl on Jan. 1, 1993, to earn the 1992 national championship?

6. Who was the leading rusher on the 1992 national championship team?

7. Which Alabama national championship team was voted as the SEC's greatest team in a 2008 vote conducted by AT&T?

8. When UA won the national championship in 1979, which Big Ten school was No. 1 in the polls heading into the bowl games?

9. What was Bama's only loss in 1978?

10. In 1973, the Tide went 11-0 in the regular season and won every game by at least 14 points. Who did they lose to in the Sugar Bowl by one point?

11. Who was the back-up quarterback on the 1965 national championship team?

12. In 1964, Bama was named the national champion before the bowl games. Who did they lose to in the Orange Bowl?

13. In 1961, the Tide allowed just 25 points in 11 games. Who was the defensive captain of that team who was the only UA player to earn All-America honors?

14. True or False? In the 1941 Cotton Bowl, Bama had just 75 yards of total offense and one first down the entire game, but beat Texas A&M, 29-21.

15. Who was Alabama's head coach for the national titles won in 1925, '26 and '30?

16. Who was Alabama's head coach for the national titles won in 1934 and '41?

17. Which No. 1 team did No. 2 Alabama beat in the Sugar Bowl to win the 1978 national championship?

18. Who was the future College Football Hall of Fame member who starred as a fullback, linebacker and punter on the 1930 national championship team?

19. Who was the member of that 1930 team who became the long-time head coach at Clemson?

20. Which UA player got thrown out of the game in the first half for unsportsmanlike conduct in the Tide's closest game (a 13-6 win over Tennessee) of their 1934 national championship season?

21. In the 2009 SEC Championship Game, who scored three touchdowns to lead UA to a 32-13 win over Florida?

22. What company is the corporate title sponsor of the SEC Championship Game?

23. Who was the leading rusher on the 1978 national championship team who started at RB for the Miami Dolphins in Super Bowls XVII and XIX?

24. Nick Saban has won national championships at two schools. Who is the only other coach to win a national title at two schools?

25. The Georgia Dome in Atlanta has been the site of the SEC Championship Game from 1994-2011. Where were the first two title games?

## Bryant Pop Up Quote

The letters in each vertical column in the grid below go into the squares directly above them, but not necessarily in the order they appear. The black squares indicate the end of a word. When you have placed all the letters in their correct positions, you will have a quotation from Bear Bryant, reading from left to right, row by row. Solution on page 135.

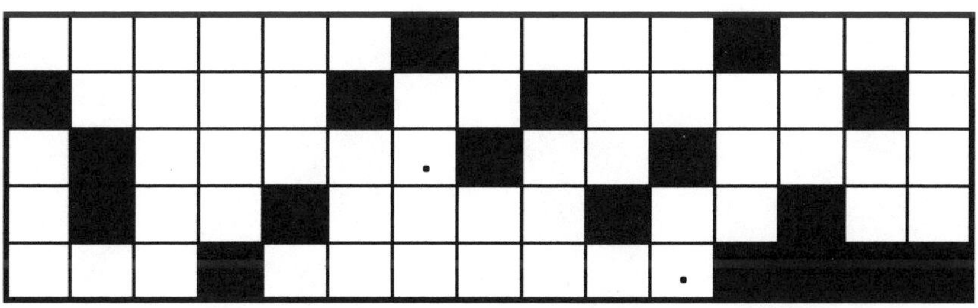

| | | | | | | | | | | | | | | |
|---|---|---|---|---|---|---|---|---|---|---|---|---|---|---|
| G | H | A | E | E | A | A | D | E | E | A | M | A | F | E |
| L | M | M | I | H | G | M | D | I | R | S | N | N | K | I |
| O | O | Q | K | I | T | R | E | O | T | T | O | T | O | T |
| S | | S | U | N | W | | N | T | W | | | | | T |
| | | T | | | | | | | | | | | | |

*Joe Namath*

## Knight Moves, Part I

On a standard 8x8 chessboard, move from square to square the way a knight moves (between opposite corners of a 2x3 rectangle) to spell the last names of the 11 offensive starters for Alabama in the BCS Championship Game following the 2009 season. (The list of starters is below.) Begin anywhere on the board and place a C (for the first letter in CARPENTER) in that square. Now move like a knight and place an A (for the second letter in CARPENTER) where you land. From there, move like a knight again and place an R in that square, and so on, until you spell CARPENTER. From the point where you end CARPENTER, continue to move like a knight a spell DAVIS and the rest of the 11 starters. Here's the tricky part: Do not use any square more than once. There are 64 letters in the starters' names and 64 squares on the board, so each and every square should be used once. If you get stumped, turn the page for an easier version of the same game. Solution on page 137.

**Starters (including two Joneses):**

CARPENTER

DAVIS

HANKS

INGRAM

JOHNSON

JONES

JONES

MAZE

MCELROY

PEEK

VLACHOS

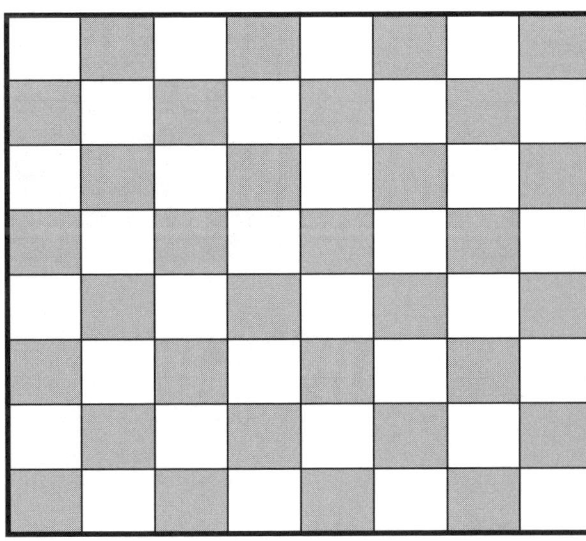

## Knight Moves, Part II

If you were not able to complete the Part I challenge, one possible solution is below. But where do you start and where do you move? That's the challenge of this puzzle. To begin, go to each C (for CARPENTER) in the grid and see which go to an A when you move like a knight. There is more than one possibility, so from each of those As, see if you can move like a knight to get to an R. Once you get started, continue to move like a knight to complete CARPENTER, then move on to DAVIS and so on, until you complete the starting lineup. Remember, do not use any square more than once. Solution is on page 137.

**Starters (including two Joneses):**

CARPENTER
DAVIS
HANKS
INGRAM
JOHNSON
JONES
JONES
MAZE
MCELROY
PEEK
VLACHOS

| | | | | | | | |
|---|---|---|---|---|---|---|---|
| K | L | L | C | C | H | G | O |
| R | A | N | A | N | S | M | S |
| V | S | P | E | A | R | H | Z |
| R | O | K | I | C | E | I | A |
| O | E | N | Y | E | M | A | A |
| O | E | N | E | E | V | N | J |
| N | J | P | S | H | O | D | M |
| E | J | T | N | R | S | O | S |

## Bama Holes

Fill in the missing letter for each of the words listed. Be careful, because each of the words can be completed with more than one letter. Transfer the correct letter to the corresponding blank so that the result is a two-word term for a very successful football team. Solution on page 136.

| ___ | ___ | ___ | ___ | ___ | ___ | ___ | ___ |
|---|---|---|---|---|---|---|---|
| 1 | 2 | 3 | 4 | 5 | 6 | 7 | 8 |

| ___ | ___ | ___ | ___ | ___ | ___ | ___ | ___ | ___ |
|---|---|---|---|---|---|---|---|---|
| 9 | 10 | 11 | 12 | 13 | 14 | 15 | 16 | 17 |

1. __OTE
2. L__NE
3. GA__E
4. CL__P
5. D__WN
6. __AME
7. FO__L
8. BAL__
9. __APE
10. T__IN
11. DAT__
12. CO__E
13. __ROM
14. F__RE
15. HER__
16. LI__T
17. __ASS

## Short Yardage Crossword

Solution on page 139.

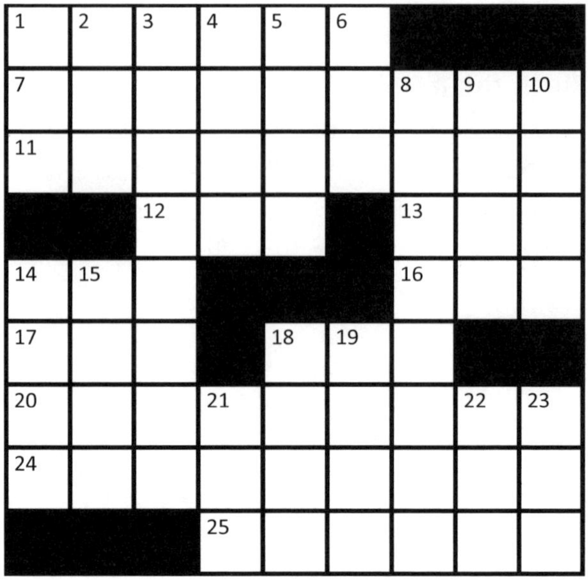

**Across**

1. Offensive MVP of the 2006 Cotton Bowl
7. It has its privileges
11. Team transports, often
12. Ichiban Japanese Grill fish
13. Rapper Dr. ___
14. PC alternative
16. Discount rack abbr.
17. Cultural Revolution leader
18. Vardalos of *My Big Fat Greek Wedding*
20. Prom flower
24. Sounded reasonable (2 wds.)
25. 1994 Johnny Unitas Golden Arm Award winner

**Down**

1. Ala. civil war side
2. King, in Portugal
3. Printed, as a quote, in *The Tuscaloosa News* (2 wds.)
4. "Goodness me!"
5. Hang out
6. Tide pitcher's stat
8. Calligrapher's purchase (2 wds.)
9. Guam, for one: Abbr.
10. Belgian river
14. XXIX x C
15. Really small battery size
18. UA-Huntsville astronaut org.
19. Old Roman road
21. New Big Ten sch.
22. Sugar suffix
23. Saul's uncle

After solving the crossword puzzle, use the letters in the grid to answer this additional clue. Transfer the letters in numbered boxes to the corresponding blanks below. (Or answer the additional clue first to help you solve the crossword puzzle.)

John Parker Wilson's back-up in 2006

___ ___ ___ ___ ___ ___
25 11 2 23 6 7

## Chapter 3

# Quarterbacks

Who is the greatest quarterback in Alabama history?

Was it Bart Starr? Joe Namath? Ken Stabler? Those three arguably enjoyed the most success as professional QBs.

Starr was UA's starter as a sophomore, leading the team to a 6-3-3 record in 1953. He completed 59-of-119 passes for 870 yards and eight touchdowns, but lost his starting spot as a junior due to a back injury. Bama made a coaching change, and new coach J.B. Whitworth wanted to prepare for the future by playing younger players. Starr spent most of his senior season on the bench as the Tide went 0-10. He wasn't drafted until the 17th round of the 1956 NFL Draft by the Green Bay Packers. When Vince Lombardi took over the Packers in 1959, he moved Starr into the starting lineup and the player and team flourished. By the time Starr concluded his pro career in 1971, he was a two-time Super Bowl MVP, five-time NFL champion, four-time Pro Bowl player and a member of the NFL 1960s All-Decade Team. Later, his uniform number 15 was retired by the Packers, and he was elected to the Pro Football Hall of Fame.

As a professional player, Joe Namath created as many headlines for his off-the-field activities as his many accomplishments on it. Sometimes lost in all the headlines was that he was a pretty good quarterback. Bear Bryant called Namath, "the greatest athlete I ever coached." Namath also had a great deal of respect for Bryant, referring to him as "not only the smartest coach I ever knew, but the man who taught me the meaning of integrity."

In Namath's sophomore season (1962), he completed 76-of-146 passes for 1,192 yards and 13 touchdowns. He added 765 yards as a junior and another 756 yards through the air as a senior. In his three-year college career, he threw for 2,713 yards with 25 TDs and 19 interceptions. He added another 655 yards on the ground. Alabama was a combined 29-4 those three years and won the national championship in 1964. Namath was the first overall pick in the AFL Draft and signed with the New York Jets. He led the Jets to the Super Bowl III title and was a five-time AFL All-Star and a two-time AFL MVP. His New York Jets uniform number 12 was retired, and he was selected to the Pro Football Hall of Fame.

Freshman Ken "The Snake" Stabler watched from the sideline as Namath and the Tide won the 1964 national championship. A year later, Stabler played little as a back-up to QB Steve Sloan as UA again won a national title. As a junior, Stabler inherited the starting spot and led Bama to an 11-0 record, including a 34-7 win in the Sugar Bowl. (However, Alabama finished third in the final polls behind Notre Dame and Michigan State.) As a senior, Stabler was kicked off the team for a while due to skipping classes and partying, and Bama fell to 8-2-1. In three seasons, Stabler completed 59 percent of his passes for 2,196 yards with 16 touchdowns and 18 interceptions. He ran for 838 yards, and UA finished 28-3-2. As a pro, Stabler was a Super Bowl champion, the NFL MVP, a four-time Pro Bowl player, and a member of the NFL 1970s All-Decade Team.

But were any of those three the greatest quarterback at Alabama? Maybe, maybe not. Some might argue that the greatest quarterback for the Tide was Jay Barker (1991-94) who led the team to a 35-2-1 record as a starter. Or John Parker Wilson (2005-08) who threw for a record 8,099 yards in his career. Or Greg McElroy (2006-10) who led Bama to the 2009 national championship and racked up a school record 2,975 yards of total offense in 2010.

Or how about the only two Alabama "quarterbacks" in the College Football Hall of Fame: John Cain (1930-32) and Riley Smith (1933-35)?

Who knows? The only certainty is that UA has been blessed with a lot of great quarterbacks.

## Mike Shula Sudoku

Use logic to fill in the boxes so every row, column and 3x3 box contains the letters M-I-K-E-S-H-U-L-A, in honor of Mike Shula. The quarterback starred for the Crimson Tide from 1983-86 and later coached at the school. Solution on page 140.

| | | | | | | A | | |
|---|---|---|---|---|---|---|---|---|
| | E | | | | A | I | | |
| K | S | | | | H | | | |
| M | | | S | | | E | U | |
| | | | H | | M | | | |
| | A | L | | | K | | | I |
| | | | K | | | | L | M |
| | | M | U | | | | S | |
| | | S | | | | | | |

## Croyle Sudoku

Use logic to fill in the grid so every row, column and 2x3 box contains the letters C-R-O-Y-L-E, in honor of Brodie Croyle. The quarterback starred for Alabama from 2002-05. Solution on page 139.

| | | L | E | | |
|---|---|---|---|---|---|
| E | Y | | | C | |
| | | | | R | E |
| O | R | | | | |
| | E | | | Y | O |
| | | R | C | | |

## QB Quote Box

| R | E | L | F |
|---|---|---|---|
| O | F | D | O |
| N | I | D | O |
| T | H | E | R |

Joe Namath was known as "Broadway Joe" and had a lengthy acting career when his playing days were over. Starting with the F in the shaded box to the right, move one square up, down, left or right (but not diagonally) and continue to move that way to spell out the Broadway show that Namath was a part of for a national tour. The show name runs continuously and uses each letter exactly once. Answers on page 141.

## Pick a Letter

Pick one letter in each pair of letters to spell out the last name of an Alabama quarterback. For example, RT AO DR DE is TODD. Answers on page 139.

1. CG AR OR RY EL ES ____________________
2. BW AE ST LT SY ____________________
3. ST HR AU LN AE ____________________
4. KR EI AT CR HI EN NT ES ____________________
5. TW OR AO DL ST NO NS ____________________
6. DS AO RV IN ST ____________________
7. SW RT AE BC LM ER RT ____________________
8. BN AR MN AE ST EH ____________________
9. DT AR AN MY KM ES EL ____________________
10. CR RU ST LN EN DT GH ES ____________________

## Quarterbacks Word Search

Solution on page 140.

| | | | | | | | | | | | | | | |
|---|---|---|---|---|---|---|---|---|---|---|---|---|---|---|
| X | W | B | Z | J | J | P | S | N | A | M | A | T | H | H |
| L | E | A | R | R | A | T | S | N | E | H | C | T | I | K |
| L | M | R | W | R | S | H | F | H | Z | N | R | Y | S | D |
| E | B | N | K | N | W | R | Q | O | O | O | O | J | L | A |
| M | C | E | L | R | O | Y | L | B | W | S | Y | L | O | V |
| M | R | S | M | D | R | T | K | S | I | K | L | E | A | I |
| A | X | N | G | E | G | N | G | O | T | C | E | W | N | S |
| R | M | R | T | G | L | N | O | N | P | A | A | I | O | K |
| T | U | N | J | I | I | A | Y | S | I | J | B | S | S | R |
| B | U | T | Y | L | K | D | S | O | D | N | B | L | L | E |
| H | O | P | L | M | C | C | A | R | R | O | N | C | E | K |
| T | E | O | A | E | D | U | N | N | C | T | O | E | N | R |
| I | H | B | E | R | D | A | W | A | T | T | S | W | P | A |
| M | N | J | H | K | O | G | J | A | L | U | H | S | C | B |
| S | W | F | S | A | T | M | E | M | O | S | L | E | Y | C |

| | | |
|---|---|---|
| BARKER | KILGROW | SHEALY |
| BARNES | KITCHENS | SHULA |
| BURGDORF | LEWIS | SLOAN |
| CROYLE | MCCARRON | SMITH |
| DAVIS | MCELROY | STABLER |
| DUNN | MOSLEY | STARR |
| GILMER | NAMATH | SUTTON |
| HOBSON | NELSON | TODD |
| HOLLINGSWORTH | PARKER | TRAMMELL |
| HUNTER | PENNINGTON | WATTS |
| JACKSON | RUTLEDGE | WOODSON |
| JACOBS | SALEM | ZOW |

## Crossing Patterns

Place the letters at the bottom of each grid into the empty squares to form the first and last names of six Alabama quarterbacks. Solutions on page 139.

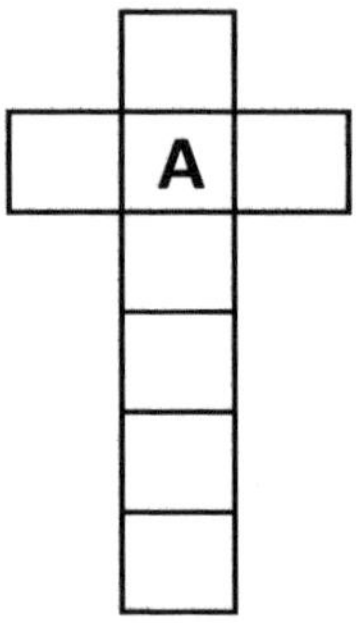


1. B E J K R R Y

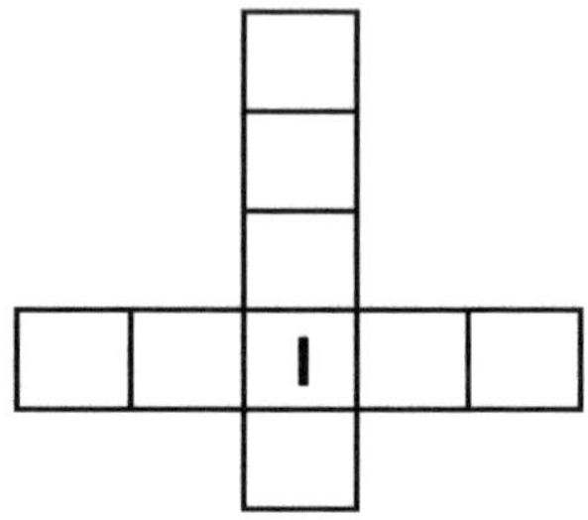


2. A D D H M S T V

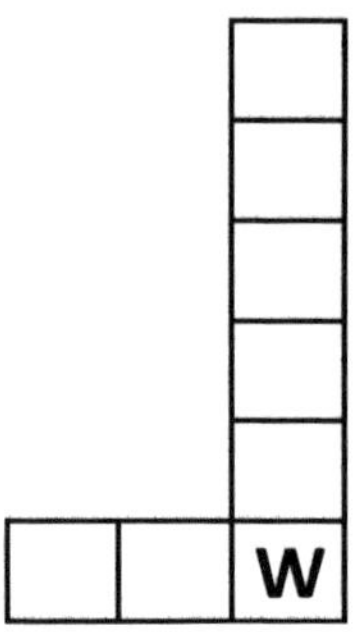


3. A D E N O R Z

4. A I L L R S T W W

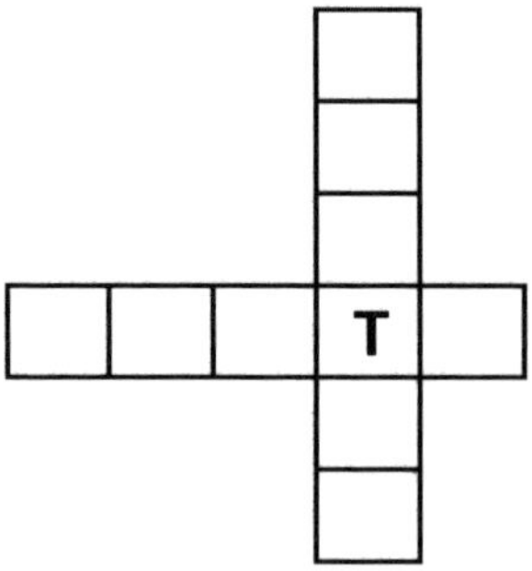


5. C E H N O R S T U

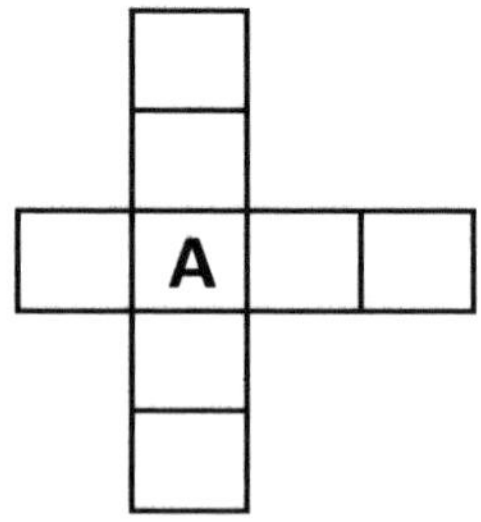


6. B R R R S T T

## Quarterbacks Trivia

Answers on page 140.

1. Which Bama All-American quarterback opened a chain of drive-ins, a travel agency and several bowling alleys with his name on them in the Birmingham area?

2. Who was the wishbone QB on the 1979 national championship team who led the team in rushing?

3. Which UA quarterback was on the cover of *Sports Illustrated* on Nov. 20, 1972, under the headline: Alabama Drives For The Top?

4. Greg McElroy graduated from UA in three years. During his undergraduate career, what kept the Academic All-American from having a 4.0 grade-point average?

5. Starting just the second game of his college career, how many consecutive passes did Greg McElroy complete to set a school record?

6. The Tide record for most total yards in a game is 457, set in 1969 vs. Auburn. Who holds that record?

7. Greg McElroy set the UA record for most total yards in a season with 2,975 in 2010. Whose record did he break?

8. Who set the school record with five touchdown passes in one game?

9. The longest pass play in UA history is 94 yards, in a 1996 game. Michael Vaughn caught the pass. Who threw it?

10. Which starting QB had the best won-loss record in his career (not counting later forfeits)?

11. Who was the quarterback on the 1961 undefeated team?

12. Who was the former UA QB who died at the age of 28 of metastatic testicular cancer shortly after earning his M.D. degree?

13. Name the former UA quarterback who went to Super Bowl XIV with the Los Angeles Rams, Super Bowl XXI with the New York Giants and Super Bowl XXVI with the Washington Redskins.

14. Which former Bama QB married the 2005 America's Junior Miss, Kelli Schutz?

15. Who wrote the book, *Crimson QB*?

16. Which former UA quarterback pleaded guilty in 2003 in a $10 million securities scam?

17. Who was the quarterback in Bear Bryant's final season?

18. Which future UA QB set the state high school shot put record at Davidson HS in Mobile?

19. Who replaced Joe Namath as the New York Jets starting QB?

20. Which UA quarterback was the lone player on the cover of the *1974 NCAA Football Record Book*?

21. Who was the Bama QB who scrambled 53 yards for the game-winning TD in a 7-3 win over Auburn in 1967 that has become known as "The Run in the Mud"?

22. Which former UA quarterback ranked 96th on *The Sporting News* list of "100 Greatest Pro Football Players" in 1999?

23. Who was the UA QB in 1964 who finally received his Alabama diploma in 2007?

24. Bart Starr was the starting quarterback for Alabama as a sophomore in 1953 and made an immediate impact. In which statistical category did he rank No. 2 in the country?

25. Which ex-UA QB is a co-host on Bama's postgame radio broadcasts?

## Quarterbacks Crossword

Solution on page 139.

**Across**

1. Mexican party animal?
7. Sports cable TV award
11. UA play part
14. Funny in a twisted way
15. *Comin' ___ the Rye*
16. Neighbor of a Vietnamese
17. "The greatest athlete I ever coached," according to Bryant
18. Locks at Three Sisters Beauty Salon
19. Word in title of first Indiana Jones film
20. Floral ring at the Hula Bowl
22. Most recent UA QB with the NY Jets
24. Ward (off)
28. TV show set at McKinley HS
30. Alabama State Police bullets and such
31. Tuscaloosa fire truck need
32. Type of shot at Walgreens
33. Center of a ball?
35. Alabama Guard group
36. Charged particles in a physics class
38. Off-center
42. Was ahead in the game
43. Pun, usually
45. State abbr.
46. Coleman Coliseum, e.g.
48. All-___ Football Classic
49. Plenty (2 wds.)
50. Bring into play
52. Sprained ankle treatment
53. Part of Alabama DOT (Abbr.)
54. Tree type in Mobile
57. "Disgusting!"
59. Sits for the school photographer
60. "The Snake"
62. Vacation spot
64. Capstone Bank convenience
65. Lake Tuscaloosa organism
67. UA QB in Green Bay between Starr and Favre
72. Once around the track at Talladega Superspeedway
73. Demeanor
74. *Seinfeld* gal
75. ___ Fields Cookies
76. Whirling water
77. Reacted to a hard tackle

**Down**

1. UA wrestler's goal
2. Bank of Tuscaloosa offering
3. ___ de plume
4. Gasteyer of *Mean Girls*
5. Championship
6. Be sore from the game
7. Biblical verb ending
8. Embarrassment over losing to Auburn
9. Tagged at University Mall
10. Bygone Tide era
11. Dorm room eye opener
12. Bama Billiards shot
13. Mirage Bowl location from 1977-93
21. Block houses
23. Places for experiments at UA
24. QB who led Bama to a 24-11-1 record from 1984-86
25. Copier need
26. Comment to the audience

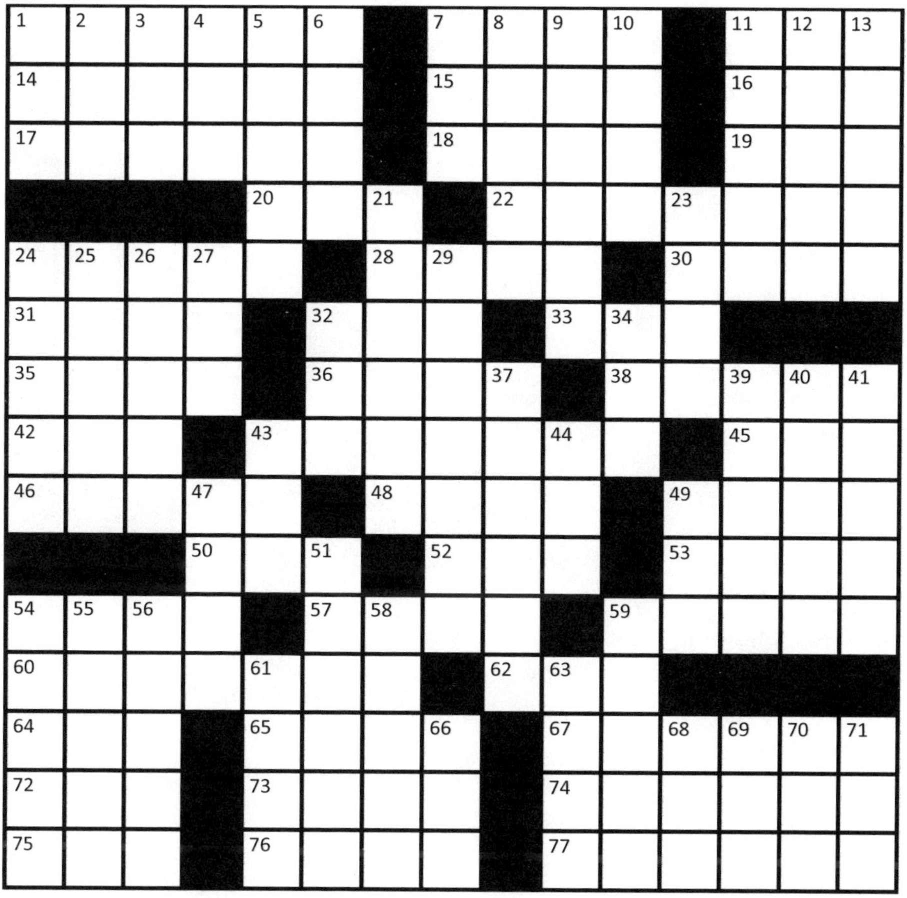

27. Bryant Drive Animal Hospital doc
29. Wacko Auburn fan
32. Evergreen
34. Tuscaloosa Farmer's Market corn serving
37. Stadium bites
39. Leafy vegetable at Piggly Wiggly
40. Skip the big wedding
41. Tide QB from 1999-2001 from Pelham, Ala.
43. Citgo product
44. State Poet Laureate's "before"
47. Feeling no pain
49. *Much ___ About Nothing*
51. Pupil protector
54. Biblical hymn
55. Fragrant oil
56. University Libraries reading lights
58. Implored
59. St. ___ Girl beer
61. Hobbling on the sidelines
63. "That was close!"
66. Unspecified number
68. A Bobbsey twin
69. ___-tac-toe
70. Chemistry class suffix
71. UA FB Lionel W. Noonan, to most

## Short Yardage Crossword

Solution on page 142.

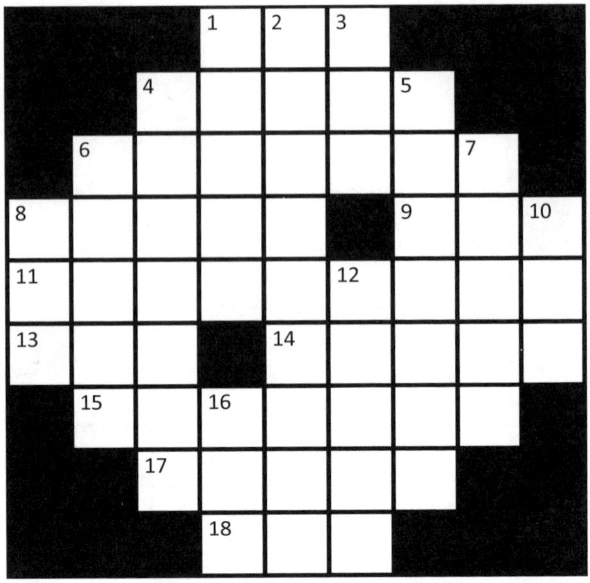

**Across**

1. Tattered Auburn uniform
4. Underneath
6. Meant to be humorous
8. Slinky's shape
9. This instant
11. Tide RB drafted 19th overall by the Seahawks in the 2000 NFL Draft, Shaun ___
13. The P of MPH
14. Down and out
15. Barnes & Noble competitor
17. Sprouts to be at the UA Arboretum
18. ___ Fields Cookies

**Down**

1. Many a dance club tune
2. Tide RB drafted in the 4th round by the Broncos in the 1998 NFL Draft, Curtis ___
3. Word on all US coins
4. Lively Spanish dances
5. Coiling plants
6. Bama VIP, briefly
7. UA women
8. Occur, old-style
10. Like some humor
12. Must-haves for all students
16. Sleep stage

After solving the crossword puzzle, use the letters in the grid to answer this additional clue. Transfer the letters in numbered boxes to the corresponding blanks below. (Or answer the additional clue first to help you solve the crossword puzzle.)

Tide RB from 1983-86 from Greensboro, Ala.

___ ___ ___ ___ ___ ___

4 16 11 3 3 17

## Chapter 4

# Running Backs

Despite Alabama's success on the field for more than 100 years, it wasn't until Mark Ingram, Jr., was named the 2009 Heisman Trophy winner that the school could claim to have the best college football player in the land.

Ingram, Jr., is the son of former NFL receiver, Mark Ingram, Sr. "Junior" was a standout running back in high school at Flint, Mich., and opted to take his skills to Alabama.

As a freshman in 2008, Ingram was a season-long back-up, but still managed to rush for 728 yards and score a team-high 12 touchdowns. As a sophomore, he ran up a school record 1,678 yards, averaging 6.1 yards per carry, and led Bama to a 14-0 record and the national championship.

Due to knee surgery in the preseason, Ingram got off to a slow start in 2010. He recovered to gain 875 yards in 11 games and added 282 yards in pass receptions. He chose to pass up his senior season to enter the NFL Draft; he was selected in the first round by the New Orleans Saints.

In accepting the Heisman Trophy, Ingram said, "I'm a little overwhelmed right now. I'm just so excited to bring Alabama their first Heisman winner. This is a great, special moment for me. Everybody that's been in the Alabama family has been supporting me. Walking to class, students flashed me the Heisman pose. I'm sure it'll be in the trophy cases with all those national championships and all the other awards people have won."

Other great running backs at Alabama include: Shaun Alexander (1996-99) who is the career rushing leader with 3,565 yards; Bobby Humphrey (1985-88) with 3,420 career yards; Kenneth Darby (2003-06) with 3,324 career yards; Johnny Musso (1969-71) with 2,741 career yards; and Dennis Riddle (1994-97) with 2,645 career yards.

Alabama running backs who have earned All-America status are: Ingram (2009), Alexander (1999), Humphrey (1986 and '87), Musso (1970 and '71), David Ray (1964), Bobby Marlow (1952), Ed Salem (1950), Harry Gilmer (1945), Joe Kilgrow (1937), James Nesbit (1936), Dixie Howell (1934), Johnny Cain (1931 and '32), John Suther (1930) and Tony Holm (1929).

Gilmer was a multi-talented back, utilizing his speed as a runner and his passing abilities. As a sophomore in 1945, he led the nation with 13 touchdown passes and ran for nine more TDs. He averaged 7.0 yards per carry and completed 65 percent of his 88 pass attempts. His 1,457 total yards ranked second in the nation as Bama finished 10-0. Gilmer was the MVP of the Tide's 34-14 Rose Bowl win over Southern Cal. He was the first overall pick in the 1948 NFL Draft and played nine seasons in the NFL. Gilmer was chosen to two Pro Bowls.

Musso was fourth in the Heisman Trophy vote as a senior in 1971, but was named the Player of the Year by *Football News*. When he finished his college career, he ranked No. 1 on Bama's career rushing list, as well as rushing TDs. His biggest games were 221 yards against Auburn in 1970 and four touchdowns against Florida in 1971. He was a two-time Academic All-American. Musso played professionally for four years, then became president of a commodities firm and a deacon in his Baptist church.

Alexander, a high draft prospect, surprised Tide fans by sticking around for a fifth season in 1999. But a sprained ankle slowed his final campaign. Still, Alexander helped lead Bama to the SEC Championship with a game-winning 25-yard TD run against No. 3 Florida in overtime. Earlier, he rolled up 199 all-purpose yards and scored three touchdowns to help Bama come from behind to beat Auburn, 28-17. He was named an All-American and selected in the first round of the 2000 NFL Draft.

## What's In a Name?

An anagram is a word, phrase or sentence formed by rearranging all the letters of another word, phrase or sentence. For example, an anagram for the name of running back EDDIE LACY is DEADLY ICE. Rearrange the letters of these anagrams to come up with the first and last names of these UA running backs. Answers on page 141.

1. THE NERDY BANK ____________________

2. ARM MARKING ____________________

3. DANISH CORNERS ____________________

4. DAMN OGRE ____________________

5. TROPHY RACK ____________________

6. CAT PURR HULA ____________________

7. CARSICK IDLERS ____________________

8. LOCKJAW BRUINS ____________________

9. ICKY ROOMER ____________________

10. SCARY SAINT ____________________

Now it's your turn. See if you can create an anagram for running back RUSS CRAFT that relates to football. (Hint: Think of what a RB gets from being tackled on artificial grass.)

## Running Backs Crossword

Solution on page 142.

**Across**

1. Bama's "Italian Stallion"
6. UA rushing leader from 1981-83, Ricky ___
11. One of five Ws at *The Crimson White*
14. Way to serve beer at The Back Porch
15. For the birds?
16. Used model at Saturn of Montgomery
17. Old enough to hit the campus bars (2 wds.)
18. WWII conference site
19. Bama FB from 1968-69, Mickey ___
20. Drop the ball at a UA baseball game
21. "Shucks!"
23. And others: Abbr.
25. Like the high dive end of the Don Gambril Olympic Pool
27. Home to Phillips University
29. Top of the recruiting class
32. Author Jong
34. Lord's Prayer start
36. Gulf Shores beach bucket
37. Antiquity, once
38. Execute a gymnastics move perfectly
40. Lady's title
41. Arab League nation
45. Quick glance
47. Cousin of an ostrich
48. Tell it to a Tuscaloosa County judge
50. 21-21, e.g.
51. TV show award
53. Thanksgiving side dish
54. Ire
57. Caught, in a way
59. Locker room powder
61. Knocked off, in a way
63. Hems' partners
65. Sounds of disdain from a coach
67. Lab eggs
68. Word said with a salute
70. Raring to go, like a new freshman
72. Escapade
74. Brewpub offering
75. Come to pass
76. It may be red?
77. Bed Bath & Beyond thickness
78. RB with five TDs in a 2002 game
79. RB with 1,242 yards in 2005

**Down**

1. Responded to a cattle call
2. Locked up
3. Unwelcome watcher from the stands
4. Hang loosely
5. *The Tuscaloosa News* section
6. Yucatan Indian
7. Big play applause
8. Castrol Express item
9. Evaluate
10. Related maternally
11. RB Shaud, Sherman or Charlie
12. Garden tool
13. Point value of a PAT
22. Without hesitation
24. Matterhorn, e.g.
26. Lake Tuscaloosa fishing spot
28. Kind of wrestling meet
30. Wear down on the field

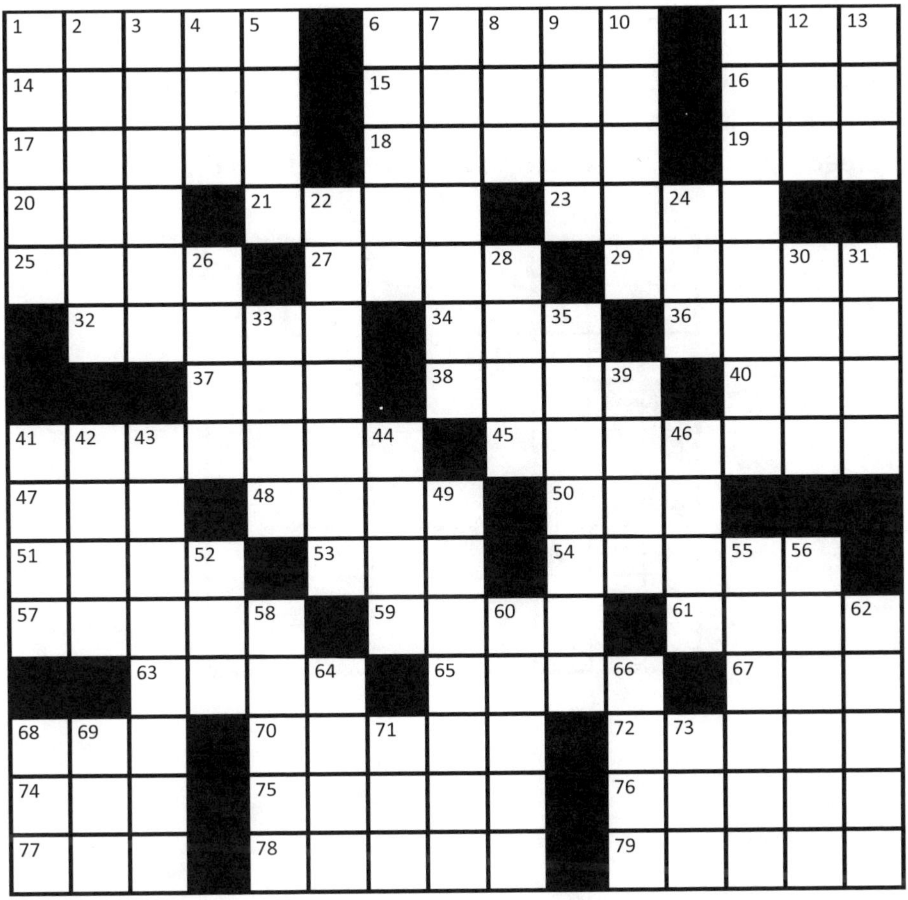

31. Ultimatum word
33. Show appreciation for a good play
35. Reading to unruly fans (2 wds.)
39. Food World butcher's cut
41. Egan's Pub brew
42. Alabama Guard supply
43. UA RB taken in the first round of the 1989 NFL Supplemental Draft
44. Tidy
46. They're tapped at frat parties
49. Pro player's opposite
52. Alabama Senate roll-call vote
55. Runaway bride or groom
56. Stadium echo effect
58. Campus geek
60. Enticed
62. Toadlike
64. Of sound mind
66. Large number
68. Talladega National Forest juice
69. Under the weather
71. Troop 88's cookie selling org.
73. State abbr.

## Tom Calvin Sudoku

Use logic to fill in the boxes so every row, column and 3x3 box contains the letters T-O-M-C-A-L-V-I-N, in honor of Tom Calvin, the leading rusher for Alabama in 1949. Solution on page 144.

| C |  |  |  |  | N |  | L |  |
|---|---|---|---|---|---|---|---|---|
|  |  | A |  | M | T |  | I | C |
|  |  | O | C | I |  | N |  | T |
| M |  |  | V |  | A | T | C | I |
|  |  |  |  | L |  |  |  |  |
| A | C | T | M |  | I |  |  | N |
| T |  | M |  | C | O | V |  |  |
| O | A |  | N | V |  | I |  |  |
|  | N |  | A |  |  |  |  | O |

## Suther Sudoku

Use logic to fill in the grid so every row, column and 2x3 box contains the letters S-U-T-H-E-R, in honor of John Suther, an All-American running back for Alabama in 1930. Solution on page 142.

|  |  | U | T | E |  |
|---|---|---|---|---|---|
|  | E | S | R |  |  |
|  |  | H |  |  |  |
|  |  |  | H |  |  |
|  |  | T | U | R |  |
|  | U | R | E |  |  |

## Double Switch

The first and last names of 10 Alabama running backs have been split into two-letter segments. The letters in each segment are in order, but the segments have been mixed up. Put together the pieces in each line to come up with the players' names. Answers on page 141.

1. NN HD ET KE BY AR ____________________
2. GA AD LL MA OW AH AY ____________________
3. ER ND XA LE NA AU SH ____________________
4. IS RI LE NN DD DE ____________________
5. TA NS SI RA CY ____________________
6. OO YM CK RE RI ____________________
7. ON AC LL BI YJ KS ____________________
8. TO NA AN TH NY ____________________
9. CU CA LL LV IV IN ER ____________________
10. MO AN RG ED ____________________

## Running Backs Trivia

Answers on page 142.

1. Which UA running back was the MVP of the 1992 Japan Bowl?

2. Mark Ingram, Sr., is in jail for what crime?

3. Mark Ingram, Jr., won the Heisman Trophy in 2009 in the closest vote in the 75-year history of the award. Who finished second?

4. Ingram won the Heisman Trophy and his school won the national championship in the same season. Who was the last player to win those titles in the same season?

5. Ingram set the UA freshman record with 12 touchdowns in 2008, even though he didn't start a game. Who was the starter at RB that year?

6. Who am I?
   * I played football at S.R. Butler HS in Huntsville.
   * At UA, I rushed for more than 1,000 yards as a sophomore and junior, earning first-team all-SEC honors.
   * As a senior in 2006, I did not have a rushing TD in 13 starts and fell just short of the school's career rushing record.

7. Where did Shaud Williams begin his college career?

8. Why did Ahmaad Galloway wear uniform number 29?

9. Who was the red-shirt freshman who ran for a school record 291 yards in a 1996 game at LSU?

10. Which UA RB led the SEC in rushing in Bama's 1961 undefeated season?

11. Who led the SEC in rushing in back-to-back seasons in 1970 and '71?

12. Which UA running back carried the ball for 15 consecutive offensive plays in a 1994 game?

13. Who holds the school career record for the highest average yards per carry (minimum of 200 carries)?

14. Who ran a school record 91 yards on one play against Temple in 1991?

15. Which Tide back was the 1987 UPI National Offensive Player of the Year and finished 10th in the Heisman Trophy vote?

16. Who was the All-American halfback who is credited with popularizing the "jump pass"?

*Mark Ingram*

17. Which former UA RB was the head coach of the Detroit Lions in 1965-66?

18. Who was Bama's leading rusher in 1985 who later claimed to have received cash to play at UA?

19. Who was the freshman who led the team in rushing in 1981?

20. Which UA running back was a second round pick in the 1978 NFL Draft and played 10 seasons in the NFL for Tampa Bay, San Francisco and Cleveland?

21. Only two UA running backs have had two 80+ yard runs in their career. One is Shaud Williams. Who is the other?

22. Who was the first African-American offered a football scholarship to attend UA in 1970?

23. Which future UA fullback was drafted out of Bullard HS (Fresno, Calif.) by the Kansas City Royals as a pitcher in the 72nd round of the 1969 MLB Draft?

24. Who was the Bama RB known as "Corky" who led the team in rushing in 1953 and '54?

25. Which UA back set the school record of 233 rushing yards in the 1951 game vs. Auburn, a record that stood for 36 years?

## Ifs and Thens

Complete this puzzle to reveal the name of an all-time great Alabama running back. Solution on page 141.

| ___ | ___ | ___ | ___ | ___ | ___ | ___ | ___ |
|---|---|---|---|---|---|---|---|
| 1 | 2 | 3 | 4 | 5 | 6 | 7 | 8 |

* If Johnny Musso was the first UA player with 1,000+ rushing yards in a season, then the 2nd letter is U; if it was Steve Bowman, then the 4th letter is L.
* If Shaun Alexander was selected in the first round of the NFL Draft by the Washington Redskins, then the 7th letter is M; if it was the Seattle Seahawks, then the 5th letter is H.
* If Ahmaad Galloway played professionally for the Scottish Claymores of NFL Europe, then the 8th letter is Y; if he played for the Toronto Argonauts of the Canadian Football League, then the 1st letter is W.
* If Dennis Riddle led the Tide in rushing yards in 1995, then the 3rd letter is M; if it was 1985, then the 6th letter is A.
* If Siran Stacy was the MVP of the 1993 Sugar Bowl, then the 2nd letter is I; if it was Derrick Lassic, then the 7th letter is E.
* If Mark Ingram wore uniform number 22, then the 6th letter is R; if he wore number 32, then the 8th letter is S.
* If Terry Grant led UA with 891 rushing yards in 2007 as a red-shirt freshman, then the 1st letter is H; if he was a fifth-year senior, then the 3rd letter is L.
* If Trent Richardson attended high school in South Carolina, then the 5th letter is I; if it was Florida, then the 4th letter is P.

## Running Backs Word Search

Solution on page 143.

| | | | | | | | | | | | | | | |
|---|---|---|---|---|---|---|---|---|---|---|---|---|---|---|
| S | L | L | A | W | T | F | A | R | C | X | N | P | Y | L |
| A | W | M | A | R | L | O | W | S | H | D | A | R | B | Y |
| L | I | K | F | O | N | M | M | G | H | R | H | A | Q | A |
| E | L | D | F | N | I | A | U | H | W | E | T | H | D | G |
| X | L | T | T | N | V | R | S | T | C | C | A | T | O | J |
| A | I | L | B | O | L | G | S | U | O | N | N | L | A | E |
| N | A | H | I | S | A | N | O | R | M | E | O | C | Y | L |
| D | M | U | S | R | C | I | A | R | S | P | K | I | C | K |
| E | S | M | C | E | P | Q | H | A | T | S | G | S | A | S |
| R | I | P | E | D | E | S | E | C | O | I | N | S | T | H |
| I | V | H | G | N | J | H | R | N | C | J | A | A | S | O |
| D | A | R | L | A | I | I | R | E | K | A | G | L | F | L |
| D | D | E | I | C | U | L | L | I | V | E | R | O | O | M |
| L | A | Y | A | W | O | L | L | A | G | G | O | F | S | X |
| E | W | O | A | N | E | L | S | O | N | A | M | W | O | B |

| | | | |
|---|---|---|---|
| ALEXANDER | DARBY | JELKS | RIDDLE |
| ANDERSON | DAVIS | LASSIC | SHEALY |
| BISCEGLIA | FRACCHIA | LOFTIN | SPENCER |
| BOWMAN | GALLOWAY | MARLOW | STACY |
| CALVIN | HILL | MOORE | TEW |
| CARRUTH | HOLM | MORGAN | THARP |
| COMSTOCK | HUMPHREY | MUSSO | VERSPRILLE |
| CRAFT | INGRAM | NATHAN | WALLS |
| CULLIVER | JACKSON | NELSON | WILLIAMS |

## Short Yardage Crossword

Solution on page 144.

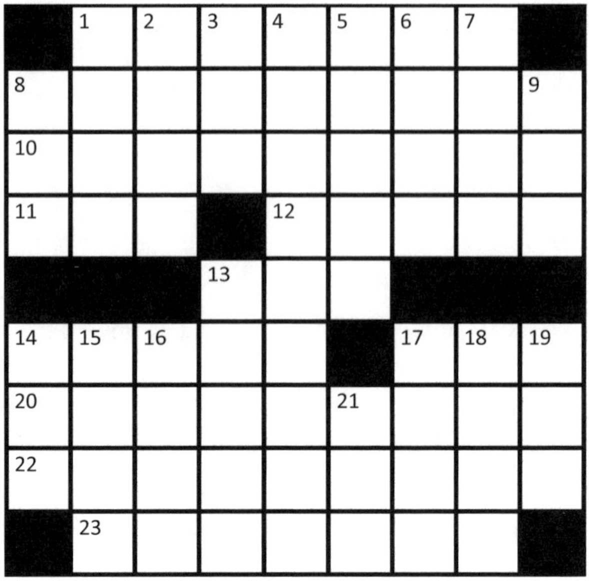

**Across**

1. Former WR who served as Grand Marshall of 2010 homecoming game
8. Fish whose name fits their look: compressed noggins
10. A continent
11. Kitchen meas. at Ruby Tuesday
12. Long jump, e.g.
13. Spelling contest
14. ___ *in Toyland*
17. Masseur's workplace, maybe
20. Comparisons
22. Annihilates the opposition
23. UA's leading receiver in 1972-73 who played one season with the Bears

**Down**

1. In addition
2. Coarse file
3. Giant Hall-of-Famer
4. Trio, like a Wishbone backfield
5. Throw a pass with effort
6. Rattled breath
7. Norse war god
8. Obese
9. Usual f'ball game day
13. Contradict
14. Spoiled
15. All over again
16. One of classical music's Three Bs
17. Game locale
18. Squint
19. Biblical beast
21. Guy's date

After solving the crossword puzzle, use the letters in the grid to answer this additional clue. Transfer the letters in numbered boxes to the corresponding blanks below. (Or answer the additional clue first to help you solve the crossword puzzle.)

WR from Rainbow City, Ala., who played from 2000-03

___ ___ ___ ___ ___
21 2 12 12 6

## Chapter 5

# Receivers

Julio Jones could have rewritten the Alabama record books. But the 2010 All-America wide receiver passed up his final season of college eligibility to enter the 2011 NFL Draft. He was selected by the Atlanta Falcons with the sixth overall pick in the first round.

In 2010, Jones caught a school record 78 passes for a school record 1,133 yards and seven TDs. After three seasons, he was in position to eclipse every Bama career receiving record in the books.

"I started playing organized football at the age of 12," Jones said. "I knew I was going to be good in my 10th grade year. I've always been a competitor growing up. I would never let anybody beat me at anything, and if they did, I was going to get my revenge."

Jones, at 6-foot-4 and 225 pounds is a prototypical big receiver. He entered Bama with considerable skills—he was the first true freshman receiver to start a season opener at UA—but he credits his experience at Alabama with elevating his game.

"We had NFL practices at Alabama. Coach Saban kind of ran an NFL program there. As far as the meetings, we were in there all day learning. Being up early, taking care of business, you have to be responsible. Coach Saban always teaches you to be accountable for your own actions. If you are late, you get punished."

Jones is the most recent in a long line of talented receivers who have gone through Alabama:

**Ozzie Newsome**—He was a four-year starter for the Tide and an All-American as a senior in 1977. He had 102 career receptions for 2,070 yards while Bama won 42 of 48 games. He was inducted into the College Football Hall of Fame. In the NFL, he was one of the top tight ends in league history. He was a three-time

Pro Bowl player and was named to the NFL 1980s All-Decade Team. In addition, he received the Whizzer White NFL Man of the Year Award for his community service and was inducted into the Pro Football Hall of Fame in 1999.

**Don Hutson**—Many historians consider Hutson the first star wide receiver in the NFL. But initially, he was a star at Alabama, earning All-America accolades as a senior in 1934 as the Tide went 10-0 and won the national championship. (He later was inducted into the College Football Hall of Fame.) He joined the Green Bay Packers in 1935, and after 11 seasons, he retired as the greatest receiver in NFL history. His uniform No. 14 was retired by the Packers, and he was elected to the Pro Football Hall of Fame.

**D.J. Hall**—He's the Alabama career leader in pass receptions (194) and career receiving yards (2,923). Despite his impressive statistics, Hall was not selected in the 2008 NFL Draft. He signed as a free agent with the New York Giants and then the Oakland Raiders, but never saw action in an NFL game. He attempted to play in the Canadian Football League, but an injury in the preseason prevented him for making the Winnipeg roster. He even had a short, but unproductive, stint in the Arena Football League. Then in 2010, Hall was arrested at a Tuscaloosa hotel and charged with first-degree possession of marijuana and possession of a controlled substance.

Other top receivers include **Al Lary** (1948-50) who had a record 10 touchdown receptions in a season; **Dennis Homan** (1965-67) who was the first Bama receiver with 50+ receptions in a season; **David Palmer** (1991-93) who averaged 15.8 yards per catch in his career; **David Bailey** (1969-71) who had 12 receptions for 150+ yards in two consecutive games against Tennessee; **Freddie Milons** (1998-2001) who had 152 career catches for 1,859 yards; **Ray Perkins** (1964-66), an All-American in 1966 who played on two of Bama's national championship teams; and **Wayne Wheeler** (1971-73) whose 22.7 yards per catch average for his career is the highest in UA history.

## McAlister Sudoku

Use logic to fill in the boxes so every row, column and 3x3 box contains the letters M-C-A-L-I-S-T-E-R, in honor of Nathan McAlister, a wide receiver on the 2010 Alabama team. Solution on page 145.

| | | | | | | | | |
|---|---|---|---|---|---|---|---|---|
| I | | S | | | | | | E |
| | M | | C | | | | R | |
| | | | | T | | | | I |
| | | | M | | T | | I | |
| | | C | | | | A | | |
| | T | | S | | L | | | |
| T | | | | L | | | | |
| | R | | | | A | | S | |
| A | | | | | | T | | C |

## Offsides Sudoku

Now use the same letters (M-C-A-L-I-S-T-E-R) and use logic to fill in the boxes so that every row and column contains those letters. The nine-letter "boxes" indicated by the solid lines aren't all square—they're offsides—but the solving rules remain the same. Solution on page 145.

| | | | | | | | | |
|---|---|---|---|---|---|---|---|---|
| | | | | S | A | | | |
| | | | | M | | T | | A |
| I | E | | | | | | R | |
| | | T | L | | | E | | |
| | | | E | | | I | | L |
| | | | R | | M | | | |
| | C | E | | | | | | |
| M | | | | | | | | I |
| | | R | | T | | | S | |

## Receivers Crossword

Solution on page 146.

**Across**

1. MIT part: Abbr.
5. Wrinkly fruit at D&G Grocery
9. Give the slip to the Alabama State Police
14. Academy of Ballet & Jazz attire
15. Provoke a visiting fan
16. Student's computer woe
17. UA Observatory sight
18. Base runner's goal
19. Fort Knox bar
20. Biology class abbr.
22. WR with 187 yards vs. Auburn in 1969
24. Turns inside out
28. It was dropped on campus in the '60s
29. Grazing ground
32. African mongooses at the Birmingham Zoo
34. Stadium grass trimmers
36. Pea's place at the Tuscaloosa Farmer's Market
37. Have a thing for the Tide
39. Facilitates
40. Puzzle theme
43. Los Tarascos restaurant bread?
46. Leak slowly
47. Kitten's cry at PetSmart
50. Toronto college
52. More soothing, as music
55. Wachovia Bank offering
56. Be sick
58. Cheered for the Tide in a half-hearted way
59. Bama's first 1,000-yard WR, in 1993
62. Antiquity, in antiquity
63. Old photo color at the Alabama History Museum
65. Jemima, for one
68. Cantina cooker
71. Player's rep
72. Blackthorn fruit
73. Tide type?
74. Rich dessert at FIG
75. Sea swallow
76. Highlander

**Down**

1. "___ show time!"
2. Cashew, e.g.
3. Famished
4. Fullback with 117 yards in receptions vs. Ole Miss in 1989
5. "That's terrible!"
6. Chang's Chinese Restaurant item: moo ___ gai pan
7. Alabama State Fair barn baby
8. Consummate
9. Villain (2 wds.)
10. Campus building climber
11. Colorful socks at Hidden Meadows Golf Course
12. ESPN radio's Mike & Mike in the morning, e.g.
13. Atlanta's winter hrs.
21. Biblical boat
23. School of thought
24. Little devil
25. *The Matrix* role
26. Uptown Barber Shop supply
27. Pigpens
30. "Able was I ___ . . ."
31. Long-eared beast
33. Skimmed the water at Lymanland

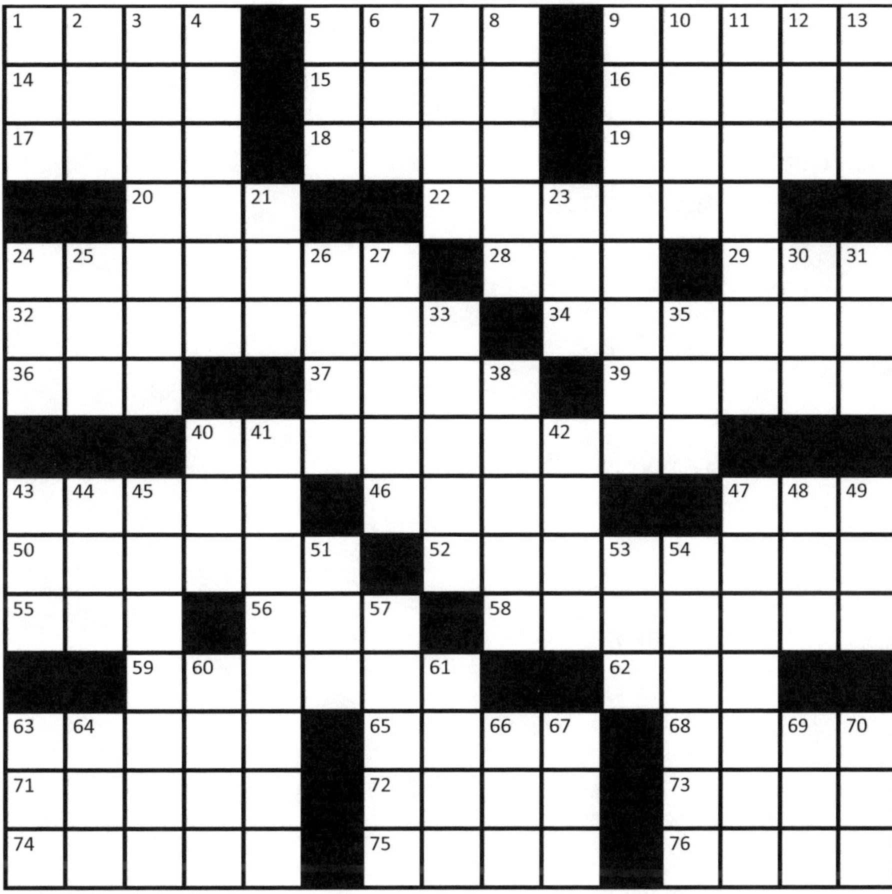

35. Used to be
38. Three-time Wimbledon winner
40. ___ *v. Wade*
41. Intensify
42. Birmingham Fencing Club weapon
43. Football air pressure meas.
44. Suffix with auction
45. Word after red and long
47. Piano student's key note (2 wds.)
48. Chuck's Fish sushi offering
49. Like some humor
51. Order between "ready" and "fire"
53. Jungle swinger
54. WR who set a school record with 152 catches from 1998-2001
57. To the lowest degree
60. "___ it the truth!"
61. Decide, as a referee
63. Usual f'ball game day
64. UA psych class topic
66. Hide-hair connector
67. Big ___ Conference
69. Thai neighbor
70. University Village address abbr.

## Dynamic Duos

The names of two pass catchers who were teammates have been combined on each line. The letters of each name are in the correct order, but you need to break apart the names to come up with the Dynamic Duos. Answers on page 144.

2010 JOHANENKS ____________ ____________

2009 MAPEZEEK ____________ ____________

2008 WAALELKXANERDER ____________ ____________

2007 MCGRCOANTY ____________ ____________

2006 BROAOWKLNEY ____________ ____________

2005 HCAADDELLLL ____________ ____________

2004 PRKNOTIGHOHT ____________ ____________

2003 LFUULGKHAEM ____________ ____________

## Who am I? Sudoku

Use logic to fill in the boxes so every row, column and 2x3 box contains the letters in the name of a memorable Alabama player. (Hint: The wide receiver is a member of the College Football Hall of Fame and Pro Football Hall of Fame.) When completed, the row indicated by the arrow will spell out his name correctly. Solution on page 144.

| | | | | | | |
|---|---|---|---|---|---|---|
| | T | | | | | O |
| | S | | N | H | | |
| ► | | | | | | |
| | N | | O | T | | |
| | | | H | U | | S |
| | U | | | | | T |

**Receivers Word Search**

Solution on page 147.

| | | | | | | | | | | | | | | |
|---|---|---|---|---|---|---|---|---|---|---|---|---|---|---|
| J | T | H | W | L | U | N | A | B | W | A | L | K | E | R |
| S | P | U | G | H | W | H | O | M | A | N | W | H | S | L |
| E | I | I | K | O | E | K | U | L | W | I | I | I | G | L |
| N | T | S | R | U | H | E | T | I | H | W | L | Q | R | E |
| O | R | B | A | F | I | L | L | N | S | L | L | E | A | B |
| J | R | D | U | M | L | Y | W | E | I | I | I | W | Y | N |
| G | E | Y | T | M | A | E | K | W | R | Y | A | R | E | P |
| P | G | E | O | P | R | O | T | H | R | O | M | W | N | E |
| A | A | S | L | P | Y | U | W | C | M | K | S | R | O | R |
| L | N | S | L | B | A | I | S | I | H | O | O | E | S | K |
| M | A | X | E | L | L | Y | L | S | M | E | N | T | K | I |
| E | R | C | S | S | I | O | N | E | E | C | R | R | C | N |
| R | K | B | O | P | N | D | P | E | A | L | N | A | A | S |
| N | D | N | N | S | N | H | G | U | A | V | L | C | J | W |
| L | L | A | H | R | I | C | H | A | R | D | S | O | N | T |

| | | | |
|---|---|---|---|
| BAILEY | HALL | NEWSOME | RUSSELL |
| BECK | HOMAN | PALMER | TOLLESON |
| BELL | JACKSON | PAYNE | VAUGHN |
| BROWN | JONES | PERKINS | WALKER |
| CARTER | KRAUT | PROTHRO | WHEELER |
| DILL | LARY | PUGH | WHITEHURST |
| DYESS | LUKE | RANAGER | WILLIAMSON |
| FLETCHER | LUNA | RAY | WILLIS |
| GRAY | MILONS | RICHARDSON | WILSON |

## Receivers Trivia

Answers on page 145.

1. Who was the Prince on Bama's 1992 national championship team?

2. Who were the two receivers with 100+ yards in pass receiving in the same game in 1999?

3. Which UA receiver is the only one with back-to-back games of 10+ receptions? Hint: He did it in 2005.

4. Who set the school record with 13 catches in a 2007 game?

5. The Bama record for most pass receiving yards in a game is 217, set in 1993. Who holds the record?

6. Who are the only three Tide receivers with 1,000+ yards in a season?

7. Who was the last UA receiver with three touchdowns in a game? (It was 1998.)

8. Which UA receiver finished third in the 1993 Heisman Trophy vote?

9. Which Tide receiver won an ESPY in 2006 for his catch of a *Hail Mary* pass vs. Southern Mississippi?

10. Which Bama receiver broke his tibia and fibula vs. Florida in 2005 and never played again?

11. Who was the former UA receiver who signed with the Eagles, Steelers, Ravens and Bengals from 2002-05, but never played in an NFL game?

12. Antonio Carter went into coaching after finishing his playing career at UA. Who was the first college coach to give him a job?

13. Who was Alabama's leading receiver in 1997 and '98 who was an Arena Football League star at Albany and played in the XFL with the Birmingham Bolts?

14. Which tight end led the Tide in pass receiving in 1989 and '90?

15. Who was the former UA TE who when he retired from the NFL in 2001 had played more games in a New York Giants uniform than anyone in history?

16. Which former UA TE won the 2004 Town of Castle Rock Celebrity Golf Tournament while a member of the Denver Broncos?

17. Which Alabama receiver went on to become the first African-American general manager of an NFL team?

18. Which Bama receiver was named the SEC Player of the Decade for the '70s?

19. Who was the team's top receiver in 1966 who earned All-America honors?

20. Who was Bama's All-American receiver who was born and raised in Muscle Shoals, Ala., and has the high school field there named in his honor?

21. Which former UA receiver led the NFL in pass receptions a record eight times while being named the league MVP twice?

22. Who was the No. 1 target of Joe Namath in his senior season in 1964?

23. Who was known as UA's "other end" when Don Hutson led Bama to the 1935 Rose Bowl?

24. Which UA receiver was known as "The Wizard of Oz"?

25. Which former Tide pass catcher became the head coach of the New York Giants and Tampa Bay Buccaneers?

## Building Blocks

Read the clues and fill in the appropriate boxes. The answer to the second clue is the answer to the first clue, plus one letter. The answer to the third clue is the answer to the second clue, plus one letter. And so on. (The order of the letters may change.) Solution on page 144.

1. Letter on the Bama logo
2. Rose Bowl area, briefly
3. Bruno's Pale ___
4. Team training table activity
5. UA campus tree
6. Tide's leading receiver, 1991-93

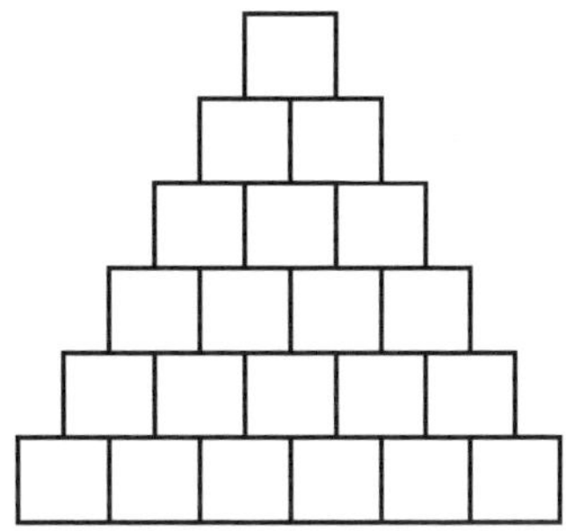

## Change a Letter

Change one letter in each word to spell the first and last names of Alabama receivers. Solution on page 145.

1. GREY WAYNE
2. COWARD CROWS
3. JOES JOKES
4. MERRY BONES
5. SAD COLLIES
6. AT BALL
7. JAMMY FILL
8. HOBBY TUNA

## Short Yardage Crossword

Solution on page 147.

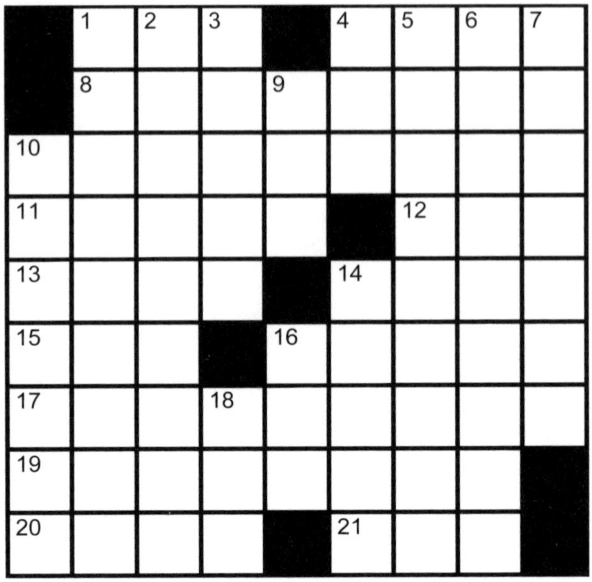

**Across**

1. Dr. J's first pro hoops league
4. Mil. addresses
8. Argentine soccer star from the 1980s and '90s
10. Capital of Israel
11. Small African antelope
12. Mont Blanc, e.g.
13. ___ run of bad luck (2 wds.)
14. Seed cover
15. Cpl. or sgt.
16. Cat-___-tails
17. Sterilizes
19. About 39 inches (2 wds.)
20. UA's Robert M. Lightfoot, Jr.'s Discovery grp.
21. Beast of burden

**Down**

1. Smithsonian stuff
2. UA Honor Choir voices
3. Caribbean cruise stop
4. Toothpaste tube letters
5. Sends to separate camps
6. Comic's zingers (2 wds.)
7. All-American OT who played from 1996-99
9. "___ was saying . . ." (2 wds.)
10. All-American OG who played from 2006-09
14. Santa ___ race track
16. Suffix with Capri
18. The Monkees' ___ *Believer* (2 wds.)

After solving the crossword puzzle, use the letters in the grid to answer this additional clue. Transfer the letters in numbered boxes to the corresponding blanks below. (Or answer the additional clue first to help you solve the crossword puzzle.)

George _______: All-American OT in 1954 who shares a name with a Fairfax, Va., university

___ ___ ___ ___ ___
8 4 17 16 20

## Chapter 6

# Offensive Linemen

It's right there in black and white (and some red and blue, too). And it comes from a credible source: *Sports Illustrated*. It was the Aug. 3, 1981, issue, and on the cover was a close-up shot of John Hannah in his football helmet. In large type over the helmet was the headline: THE BEST OFFENSIVE LINEMAN OF ALL TIME.

In the *SI* story, New England Patriots general manager Bucko Kilroy had this to say about Hannah: "For all his size and explosiveness and straight-ahead speed, John has something none of the others ever had, and that's phenomenal, repeat, phenomenal lateral agility and balance, the same as defensive backs. You'll watch his man stunt around the opposite end, and John will just stay with him. He'll slide along like a toe dancer, a tippy-toe. And that's a 270-pound man doing that, a guy capable of positively annihilating an opponent playing him straight up."

That's the same John Hannah who was an All-American guard at Alabama from 1970-72. And the same Hannah family that produced Herb Hannah, a dairy farmer who started for the New York Giants as a 30-year old rookie in 1951 after playing at Alabama, Bill Hannah, a starting guard for Alabama from 1957-59, and John's two younger brothers: Charley, an offensive lineman at UA from 1974-76 and David, a defensive lineman at Alabama from 1975-79.

More praise for John Hannah came from Bear Bryant: "He was the greatest lineman I ever coached."

Hannah was an All-Pro for 10 consecutive seasons (1976-85), played in the Pro Bowl nine times, and was a member of the NFL 1970s All-Decade Team *and* the NFL 1980s All-Decade Team. He was inducted into the Pro Football Hall of Fame in 1991, the first New England Patriots player to be enshrined. When told that he had been elected to the HOF, Hannah said, "I've never had a moment like this in my life. I cannot describe how I feel. I'm shaking. I feel like just laughing, it feels so good. It is the fulfillment of my lifetime dream. I have hoped for a long time for this moment, and now that it is here, I still can't quite believe it."

Hannah was inducted into the College Football Hall of Fame in 1999.

Another Alabama offensive lineman who gained national recognition was All-American Fred Sington (1929 and '30). Sington was elected to the College Football Hall of Fame, but his notoriety comes from being the subject of a Rudy Vallee song, titled *Football Freddie,* that became a national hit. Sington also was an outfielder for six years in the Major Leagues with the Washington Senators (1934-37) and Brooklyn Dodgers (1938-39), retiring with a .271 career batting average. He served as a Lt. Commander in World War II, then after the war became a successful businessman in Birmingham. In addition, he was a long-time SEC football official. At UA, he was a Phi Beta Kappa student and was awarded an honorary Doctor of Humane Letters degree from the University in 1976. The Birmingham native died in 1998 at the age of 88.

Other Alabama offensive linemen who received All-America honors are Mike Johnson (2009), Andre Smith (2008), Antoine Caldwell (2008), Chris Samuels (1999), Larry Rose (1988), Dwight Stephenson (1979), Jim Bunch (1979), Sylvester Croom (1974), Buddy Brown (1973), Jim Krapf (1972), Alvin Samples (1969), Cecil Dowdy (1966), Richard Dole (1966), Paul Crane (1965), Dan Kearley (1964), Wayne Freeman (1964), Lee Roy Jordan (1962), George Mason (1954), Vaughn Mancha (1945), Don Whitmire (1942), Joe Damnanovich (1942), Carey Cox (1939), James Ryba (1937), Leroy Monsky (1937), Arthur White (1936), Bill Lee (1934), Tom Hupke (1933), Fred Pickhard (1926) and W.T. VandeGraaff (1913).

## J.B. Closner Sudoku

Use logic to fill in the boxes so every row, column and 3x3 box contains the letters J-B-C-L-O-S-N-E-R, in honor of J.B. Closner, a center for Alabama from 2003-05. Solution on page 149.

| S | | | | N | | | | C |
|---|---|---|---|---|---|---|---|---|
| | | | R | | O | | | |
| | | J | | E | | B | | |
| | R | | | | | | N | |
| N | | C | | | | S | | J |
| | L | | | | | | E | |
| | | R | | S | | E | | |
| | | | C | | J | | | |
| O | | | | L | | | | R |

## Howard Sudoku

Use logic to fill in the grid so every row, column and 2x3 box contains the letters H-O-W-A-R-D, in honor of Alabama lineman Frank Howard, a member of the College Football Hall of Fame. Solution on page 147.

| W | | | | | |
|---|---|---|---|---|---|
| | | H | O | | R |
| H | | O | R | | W |
| D | | W | H | | A |
| O | | A | W | | |
| | | | | | O |

## O-Line Name Grid

These offensive linemen's names are listed in alphabetical order according to length. Fit them into their proper places in the grid. We've started your solving by placing the name CARRIGAN in the grid. Now look for a 6-letter name that has a C as the fourth letter. Continue working that way until you've filled in the grid. But be careful. There might be a name that seems to work in more than one place, but each name is used just once. Solution on page 148.

| 4 Letters | 5 Letters | 6 Letters | 7 Letters |
|---|---|---|---|
| KING | ATLAS | CONDON | CHATMAN |
| MOTT | BROCK | COWELL | CLOSNER |
| PUGH | BUNCH | CRYDER | COCHRAN |
| ROSE | DAVIS | DRAPER | DISMUKE |
| ZUGA | HOGAN | FOSHEE | EPHRAIM |
| | HURST | HANNAH | JOHNSON |
| | KRAPF | MANCHA | REDMILL |
| | LAUER | RAINES | SAMPLES |
| | MARTZ | SHEILS | WOZNIAK |
| | SHIPP | SMILEY | |
| | SMITH | WILSON | |

C A R R I G A N

## Offensive Line Crossword

Solution on page 149.

**Across**

1. OT who was 1st overall pick in 1997 NFL Draft
5. Way too weighty, like a seldom used O-lineman
10. Jell-O shaper
14. Discontinued GM line
15. Fraternity escapade
16. Opera highlight
17. Database command
18. Aegean vacation locale
19. Get misty-eyed over a Tide loss
20. However, informally
21. Bama highlights location: You___
22. Associate
24. UA OT who was 3rd overall pick in 2000 NFL Draft
26. Needle case
27. Warmed the bench
28. Kilt wearers
32. Nike shoestrings
35. A "D" at UA
36. State abbr.
37. Wear away the bank of the North River
38. Apiece, in scores
39. Taco Casa chip dip
41. Turkish title
42. Super Bowl featuring Miami and Minnesota
43. "Come here ___?"
44. Certain hunting dog
47. Gilda's of the Galleria, e.g.
48. Equipment manager's hole-making tools
49. UA O-lineman who played for the Eagles, Dolphins and Browns in the NFL from 2003-06
53. Former game in Houston: Blue___ Bowl
56. Colored eye part
57. Org. that may say no to drugs
58. "Once ___ a time . . . "
59. Open, in a way
61. In ___ of (replacing)
62. Volcanic flow
63. Poker ploy
64. Face-to-face exam at UA
65. Unexciting
66. Wrapped up practice
67. Doug's Beauty Salon goops

**Down**

1. Roll 'Bama Roll blog entries
2. Hawaii's former game: ___ Bowl
3. PC drive insert
4. Charlotte's winter hrs.
5. Supernatural
6. Alabama farm fence features
7. Olympic weapon
8. UA tennis team match part
9. ___ set: building toy
10. UA OT/G who played for Panthers, Dolphins and Bengals in the NFL from 2005-10
11. Piggly Wiggly black and white cookie buy
12. Tall tale teller
13. It might be thrown at Houndstooth Sports Bar
21. Annoy persistently
23. Ump's call at Sewell-Thomas Stadium
25. Brought into play
26. Dangerous bacteria
28. Firm

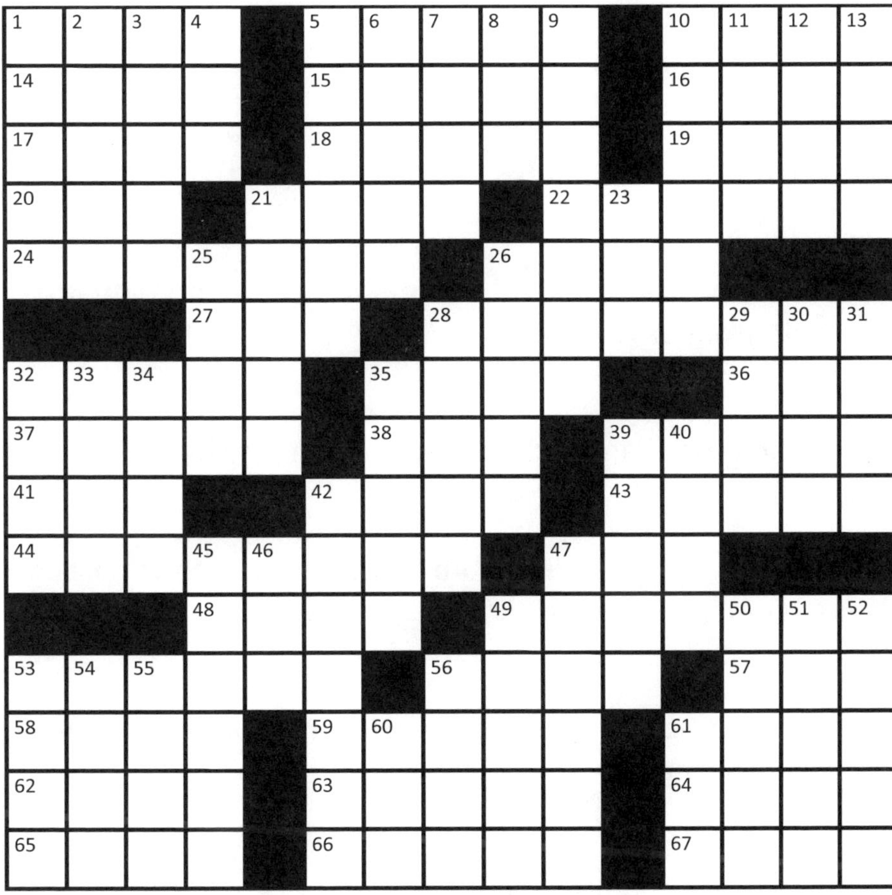

29. Soda fountain treat
30. "If all ___ fails . . ."
31. Bread at Sitar Indian Cuisine
32. Fall faller on campus
33. Jason's ship
34. Gently persuade
35. Aches' counterparts
39. Frosh, next year
40. Way, way off, like Huntsville
42. Buzzard relative
45. All-American OT who was on the UA wrestling and track & field teams, too
46. See red?
47. Like the Holy Spirit Catholic Church
49. Clear the locker room chalkboard
50. In flames
51. Archetype
52. Manhandles the opposition
53. Bryant-Denny Stadium lights insert
54. UA All-American OT Buddy Brown's October birthstone
55. Alabama PBS science show
56. UA term paper footnote abbr.
60. Bert Bobbsey's twin
61. Cabin material at Oak Mountain State Park

## Offensive Line Trivia

Answers on page 150.

1. Who was the Tide left tackle who scored a touchdown on a pitch play in the 2006 Independence Bowl?

2. Which NFL team did John Hannah play his entire pro career with from 1973-85?

3. Which NFL teams did Charley Hannah play for?

4. Which UA All-Century Team offensive lineman was killed in a hunting accident in Arkansas in 2002?

5. Who did Bear Bryant call, "the finest blocking tackle we've ever coached"?

6. Which NFL team selected All-American guard Mike Johnson in the 2010 NFL Draft?

7. Who is the only offensive lineman to win Alabama's high school "Mr. Football" award?

8. Who was the player who started games at tackle, guard and center from 2005-08 who got his degree in under three years, becoming the first Bama football player to do that?

9. Which UA tackle was the third overall pick in the 2000 NFL Draft (by Washington)?

10. Which Bama All-American lineman became the first African-American head coach in the SEC (at Mississippi State)?

11. Who was the All-American guard who was captain of the 1937 Tide team that played in the '38 Rose Bowl?

12. Which former UA tackle was chosen to the NFL's 1930s All-Decade Team?

13. A total of seven players started at the five offensive line positions over the course of the 2010 season. Name five of those players.

14. Which O-lineman won the 2010 Jerry Duncan "I Love to Practice" Award?

15. UA center William Vlachos was coached at Mountain Brook High School by which former Tide standout wide receiver?

16. Which Bama guard was a first-team Academic All-American in 2010?

*John Hannah*

17. Which Tide offensive lineman in 2010 was the son of a former UA basketball player?

18. Which Alabama lineman was named a Freshman All-American in 2010?

19. Which O-line starter in 2010 recovered a fumble as a freshman defensive lineman in his first game at Bama in 2007?

20. Who was Alabama's offensive line coach in the 2011 season?

21. Which UA lineman was the 25th pick in the first round of the 2011 NFL Draft?

22. Who was the O-line captain on the 1992 national championship team?

23. Which Bama lineman in 1977-79 was named to the Pro Football Hall of Fame after a standout career with the Miami Dolphins from 1980-87?

24. Who are the only two O-linemen from UA to play in the Japan Bowl? One was a center in 1987 and the other a guard in 1989.

25. Who is Alabama's spring practice award for Most Improved Offensive Lineman named in honor of?

## Offensive Line Word Search

Solution on page 148.

| | | | | | | | | | | | | | | |
|---|---|---|---|---|---|---|---|---|---|---|---|---|---|---|
| E | S | N | E | N | S | S | F | E | C | R | Y | D | E | R |
| K | L | A | X | O | H | M | R | B | O | K | U | Y | C | D |
| P | L | G | M | M | E | C | A | N | C | U | A | S | A | A |
| U | E | O | N | P | I | C | N | E | H | H | Y | E | R | V |
| H | W | H | A | O | L | L | C | G | R | C | D | N | R | I |
| S | O | Z | E | U | S | E | I | R | A | M | E | I | I | S |
| L | S | T | E | V | E | N | S | O | N | I | L | A | G | P |
| J | T | L | K | P | I | D | E | M | G | S | E | R | A | O |
| L | A | U | E | R | K | O | S | H | E | A | T | T | N | R |
| N | T | H | A | U | I | N | B | U | P | R | T | M | O | T |
| W | U | S | R | K | M | O | R | R | H | E | E | B | D | I |
| O | M | H | L | K | R | A | P | F | R | G | T | U | N | S |
| R | O | I | E | S | O | R | S | S | A | Q | G | S | O | D |
| B | T | P | Y | Y | D | W | O | D | I | I | R | I | C | E |
| W | T | P | H | A | N | N | A | H | M | O | O | R | C | D |

| | | |
|---|---|---|
| AYDELETTE | GERASIMCHUK | RAINES |
| BROWN | HANNAH | RICE |
| CARRIGAN | HOGAN | ROSE |
| COCHRAN | HUPKE | SAMPLES |
| CONDON | KEARLEY | SAMUELS |
| CROOM | KRAPF | SHEILS |
| CRYDER | LAUER | SHIPP |
| DAVIS | MCCLENDON | SHULTZ |
| DOWDY | MOTT | SOWELL |
| EPHRAIM | NEIGHBORS | STEPHENSON |
| FRANCIS | PATTERSON | STEVENSON |
| FRUHMORGEN | PORTIS | TATUM |

## Fill the Grid

It's your turn to be a crossword puzzle constructor. Using the name RAY in the diagonal (in honor of center Michael Ray, a letterman for UA from 1995-97), complete the grid with three three-letter words (or names or abbreviations common in crossword puzzles) going across that also make three three-letter words (or names or abbreviations) going down. There are several possible solutions. Ours is on page 149.
If you need help, here's a hint: The six letters we used to fill our grid were D, E, O, R, R, T.

| R | | |
|---|---|---|
| | A | |
| | | Y |

---

Now try one a bit tougher. Using the name SIGN in the diagonal (in honor of Chris Sign, a guard who lettered for UA in 1997), complete the grid with four four-letter words (or names or abbreviations common in crossword puzzles) going across that also make four four-letter words (or names or abbreviations) going down. There are a few possible solutions. Ours is on page 149. If you need help, here's a hint: The 12 letters we used to fill our grid were A, A, D, D, E, E, E, G, H, L, L, T.

| S | | | |
|---|---|---|---|
| | I | | |
| | | G | |
| | | | N |

## Short Yardage Crossword

Solution on page 150.

**Across**

1. LB who transferred to Central Washington after the 2008 season
5. 360-pound DT who earned All-America honors in 2008 and '09
9. Part of the eye
10. Ancient theaters
11. Start of a counting-out rhyme
12. Bit of smoke
13. "Crosses the Ts" partner (3 wds.)
15. Unreturnable serve from the UA tennis team
16. Fair chance (2 wds.)
22. Anger the ref, with "up"
23. Start of the 8th century
24. Beatnik's "Got it" (2 wds.)
25. ___ *Brockovich*
26. DB from 2005-09 whose father also played at UA
27. LB who was picked by the Vikings in the 1st round of the 1997 NFL Draft

**Down**

1. Tinted
2. Tuscaloosa Chevrolet model
3. Mardi Gras follower
4. Comes up empty (3 wds.)
5. Ranch hand, often
6. *Garfield* dog
7. *I Love Lucy* husband
8. Tuscaloosa Animal Control pound sounds
14. Frozen yogurt place: ___Y
16. Estrada of *CHiPs*
17. "Veni, ___ vici"
18. Tiger's ex-wife
19. Hosiery shade
20. Batteries Plus fluid
21. Warm-hearted

After solving the crossword puzzle, use the letters in the grid to answer this additional clue. Transfer the letters in numbered boxes to the corresponding blanks below. (Or answer the additional clue first to help you solve the crossword puzzle.)

DE who hugged NFL commissioner Paul Tagliabue when he was drafted in 1993

___ ___ ___ ___ ___
5 9 22 27 8

## Chapter 7

# Defensive Players

If there ever were a school that deserved the title of "Linebacker U", it's the University of Alabama. After all, Bama has churned out more Hall of Fame, All-America and All-Pro linebackers than any college in the nation.

The first linebacker at UA to receive national recognition was Lee Roy Jordan. Bear Bryant said, "He was one of the finest football players the world has ever seen. If runners stayed between the sidelines, he tackled them. He never had a bad day. He was 100 percent every day in practice and in the games."

The two-way star (center and linebacker) was an All-American in 1962. In his final game wearing a Bama uniform, he unofficially recorded 31 tackles in a 17-0 Orange Bowl win over Oklahoma. Jordan was inducted into the College Football Hall of Fame. As a pro, Jordan played 14 seasons for the Dallas Cowboys. He was a five-time Pro Bowl player and the 1973 NFL Defensive Player of the Year. The Cowboys played in three Super Bowls and five NFC Championship Games in his tenure. In 1989, he became the seventh player included in the Cowboys Ring of Honor.

Bama linebacker Mike Hall continued the tradition in earning All-America honors in 1968, followed by Woodrow Lowe in 1973, '74 and '75. Following his stellar career at UA, Lowe played 11 years for the San Diego Chargers. He missed just one game in his career and retired with 21 interceptions and 15 quarterback sacks. Lowe was inducted into the College Football Hall of Fame in 2009.

Next came Barry Krauss, an All-American in 1978, and Thomas Boyd, an All-American in 1980 and '81. At the same time, E.J. Junior was earning All-America honors on his way to a standout NFL career. He was a two-time Pro Bowler.

Cornelius Bennett was a three-time All-American (1984, '85 and '86) and the second overall pick in the 1987 NFL Draft. He was a five-time Pro Bowl player, the AFC Defensive Player of the Year (1988) and a member of the NFL 1990s All-Decade Team. He was inducted into the College Football Hall of Fame in 2005.

Derrick Thomas was an All-American for the Tide in 1988 and the fourth overall pick in the 1989 NFL Draft. He set an NFL record with seven sacks in a game. Thomas was a nine-time Pro Bowl selection and a member of the NFL 1990s All-Decade Team. In his career, he had 19 fumble recoveries, 126.5 quarterback sacks and three safeties. The Kansas City Chiefs retired his uniform number 58, and he was inducted into the Pro Football Hall of Fame. Thomas died in 2000 at the age of 33 from a massive blood clot related to injuries from an automobile accident.

Keith McCants was an All-American in 1989 and the fourth overall pick in the 1990 NFL Draft. Said Kentucky coach Jerry Claiborne: "Keith is one of the best football players I have ever seen. Have you ever seen a linebacker as big as he is? I never have. He looks like an elephant, and he runs like a deer."

Dwayne Rudd made the All-America team in 1996 and was a first round NFL Draft pick, followed by DeMeco Ryans in 2005. Ryans was the SEC Defensive Player of the Year and the NFL Defensive Rookie of the Year. He is also a two-time Pro Bowl player.

The most recent Bama LB with All-American next to his name is Rolando McClain. He won the Butkus Award in 2009, given to the nation's most outstanding college linebacker. He was the eighth overall pick in the 2010 NFL Draft and signed a reported $40 million, five-year contract with the Oakland Raiders.

Besides great linebackers, the Tide has had 27 other defenders chosen to All-America teams. Safety Mark Barron was named to the 2010 AA squad, cornerback Javier Arenas made the 2009 team, safety Rashad Johnson was a 2008 pick and defensive tackle Terrence Cody made the 2008 and '09 AA teams.

## Baumhower Sudoku

Here's a Sudoku that is missing the clues, in honor of Bob Baumhower, Alabama's leading tackler in 1975 and '76. He went on to play 10 seasons with the Miami Dolphins, earning a spot in the NFL Pro Bowl five times. Place the nine completed 3x3 boxes in the blank grid so that every row and every column contains the letters B-A-U-M-H-O-W-E-R. There are several possible solutions; ours is on page 150.

| B | A | U |
|---|---|---|
| O | M | R |
| H | E | W |

| W | R | E |
|---|---|---|
| U | H | B |
| O | A | M |

| R | O | U |
|---|---|---|
| H | E | A |
| M | B | W |

| M | A | H |
|---|---|---|
| O | W | E |
| B | R | U |

| M | W | B |
|---|---|---|
| R | U | O |
| E | H | A |

| H | O | M |
|---|---|---|
| A | E | W |
| U | B | R |

| E | H | A |
|---|---|---|
| W | M | B |
| R | U | O |

| W | R | E |
|---|---|---|
| U | B | H |
| A | O | M |

| B | U | O |
|---|---|---|
| A | M | R |
| E | W | H |

| | | | | | | | | |
|---|---|---|---|---|---|---|---|---|
| | | | | | | | | |
| | | | | | | | | |
| | | | | | | | | |
| | | | | | | | | |
| | | | | | | | | |
| | | | | | | | | |
| | | | | | | | | |
| | | | | | | | | |

## Defensive Players Crossword

Solution on page 151.

**Across**

1. Like some of the books at The Book Rack
5. Knocks for a loop
10. Hot springs
13. No longer around
14. Atlantic or Pacific
15. Threadbare, as some old practice gear
16. Prospector's find
17. Birmingham Zoo heavyweight
18. Totally botch
19. To the extreme (2 wds.)
21. From what place
23. Norm at the UA Golf Course
24. Stretchy fabric at the UA Recreation Center
25. Invisible
29. DT with 13 sacks in 1996, Michael ___
30. UA Arboretum potting need
31. Glows around Tide stars
32. Start of a Bama cheer: "Gimme ___!" (2 wds.)
35. Mix-up
37. African antelope
38. Comedy Club specialty
40. Sleep stage
41. Civil rights org. formed in 1909
43. Unwanted e-mail
44. LB with school-record 16 sacks in 1998, Trevis ___
45. Cheap
47. Out of it
50. First baseman, to Abbott and Costello
51. Disagreeable encounters
52. A type of parallelogram
57. Smile
58. Manner of speaking
60. Tuscaloosa Symphony Orchestra woodwind
61. Latin 101 word at UA
62. Drink served with marshmallows
63. rolltide.com, e.g.
64. "What did I tell you?"
65. What serious players play for
66. Lead player

**Down**

1. Aptly named fruit
2. Any day now
3. Mike Pitts and Eric Curry, e.g.
4. Like Marguerite Harbert's pockets
5. UA LB who is on the Dallas Cowboys Ring of Honor
6. Shade of yellow
7. Aloha Bowl garlands
8. Go for the bronze at Planet Beach?
9. Tuscaloosa Farmer's Market veggie (2 wds.)
10. In good shape
11. UA coach fired in 2003 without coaching a game
12. Off-site UA Library facility
15. Small songbirds
20. *Tarzan* extra
22. Like Siberian winters
24. IHOP pancake topper
25. The Beatles' *Back in the* ___
26. All's opposite
27. Thailand, once
28. Santa's helper

29. Chew (on)
31. Tiny type size in *The Tuscaloosa News*
32. Tuscaloosa Amphitheater concert equipment
33. LB Miller or T Langdale
34. 1988 Sun Bowl opponent
36. Sap of courage
39. Mobile coll.
42. Not feeling well on a team flight
44. Alabama State Fair barn
45. UA LB who won the Butkus Award in 1988
46. CD-___
47. Prods
48. Bryce Hospital worker
49. Licoricelike flavor
50. Shout following a Bama win
52. Conference USA school
53. Head honcho
54. Brief bio, on parting
55. UA fraternity letter
56. Animal on I-20 XING signs
59. Female variety of 56-Down

## LOWE Combos

Woodrow Lowe set an Alabama school record with 134 tackles in 1973. The linebacker went on to play 11 seasons in the NFL with the San Diego Chargers. The letters L-O-W-E can be arranged to form 24 different combinations. Here are 21 of those combinations. Which three combinations are missing? Answer on page 152.

| | | | | | | |
|---|---|---|---|---|---|---|
| OLEW | LOEW | WLOE | WELO | WOEL | OLWE | OEWL |
| EWOE | EOLW | LOWE | LWEO | EOWL | WEOL | LWOE |
| WOLE | OWEL | ELWO | OWLE | LEOW | EWEO | OELW |

## Build the Names

Use the letter groups—one at the beginning and one at the end—to build the names of former UA defensive stars. Each letter group will be used once. Solutions on page 152.

| | | | | | | | | | |
|---|---|---|---|---|---|---|---|---|---|
| AND | ANT | CAS | CON | COP | DON | ELL | ERS | GIL | IES |
| JEF | LLE | LLY | MIL | MIT | NER | RRY | SAU | SON | THO |

1. ___ TI ___
2. ___ CH ___
3. ___ NE ___
4. ___ BE ___
5. ___ EL ___
6. ___ MP ___
7. ___ FR ___
8. ___ LI ___
9. ___ ND ___
10. ___ ST ___

## Defensive Players Word Search

Solution on page 151.

| | | | | | | | | | | | | | | |
|---|---|---|---|---|---|---|---|---|---|---|---|---|---|---|
| T | N | O | C | A | B | O | D | Q | B | M | B | J | H | P |
| H | C | L | A | R | K | F | A | N | L | L | R | F | B | I |
| O | Y | S | E | L | Y | L | R | N | A | O | O | N | R | T |
| M | K | R | A | U | S | S | E | E | I | H | W | O | A | T |
| A | G | W | R | T | R | C | W | P | R | F | N | S | G | S |
| S | R | M | S | U | N | Z | O | O | S | I | F | N | G | T |
| R | O | C | I | I | C | I | H | P | N | E | H | I | S | E |
| E | I | N | T | A | R | S | M | I | E | A | N | B | R | A |
| C | N | E | U | V | R | R | U | Z | L | L | N | O | Q | G |
| N | U | A | D | E | M | R | A | L | O | O | A | R | J | U |
| E | J | L | T | U | E | J | B | H | T | N | P | N | S | E |
| P | R | L | G | K | K | D | X | R | X | D | D | I | D | P |
| S | A | N | R | D | O | E | U | S | N | O | Y | L | R | V |
| W | A | A | P | N | U | B | S | H | E | N | I | L | C | T |
| M | P | P | S | I | V | R | A | J | N | O | S | L | E | N |

| | | | |
|---|---|---|---|
| BACON | CURRY | JUNIOR | PARKER |
| BAUMHOWER | DUKES | KRAUSS | PITTS |
| BLAIR | GRIFFIN | LONDON | POPE |
| BRAGGS | HALL | LYLES | ROBINSON |
| BROWN | HAND | LYONS | SPENCER |
| BURTON | HARRIS | MANGUM | TEAGUE |
| CLARK | HOLM | MCNEAL | THOMAS |
| CLINE | JARVIS | NELSON | TRIPOLI |
| COPELAND | JONES | OZMINT | WALTERS |

## Defensive Players Trivia

Answers on page 152.

1. Who was the first African-American to play in a game for the Tide?

2. Which future UA head coach had 20 tackles and a fumble recovery against Tennessee in 1974 and was named the SEC Defensive Lineman of the Week?

3. Which cornerback ended his UA career with three interceptions in the 1982 Liberty Bowl in Bear Bryant's last game?

4. Which two Tide linebackers were named to the Walter Camp Football Foundation All-Century Team?

5. Which linebacker was a co-captain on the 1992 national championship team?

6. Who recorded eight tackles, batted down a pass and had three QB sacks (including one for a safety) in Bama's 8-3 win over Penn State in 1988, prompting CBS announcer Brent Musburger to say, "the most dominating performance I have ever seen by a college player"?

7. Who was the All-American safety arrested in Mobile for second degree hindering prosecution relating to an auto accident two days before the start of 2011 spring practice?

8. Which All-American defensive lineman spent two years at Mississippi Gulf Coast Community College before enrolling at UA in 2008?

9. Who am I?
   * I played at Sulligent High School.
   * I had no Division I scholarship offers and walked-on at UA.
   * I had three interceptions at LSU in 2008 and was named an All-American that year.
   * I was drafted by the Arizona Cardinals in 2009 and have played two years there.

10. Who was the 2005 SEC Defensive Player of the Year and the defensive MVP of the 2006 Cotton Bowl?

11. Which two UA defensive standouts, who both played in the NFL, were teammates at South Panola High School in 1993?

12. Which former Bama defensive back is one of only two players to play with the original Cleveland Browns (1994-95) and the expansion Cleveland Browns (in 1999)?

13. Who were the two "bookends" that anchored the defensive line for the 1992 national championship team?

14. Who was named the National Defensive Player of the Year by CBS in 1989?

15. Who was the Bama player recruited as a wishbone quarterback who earned All-America honors in 1981 and '82 as a defensive back?

16. Who was selected the 1975 SEC Defensive Player of the Year and Defensive MVP of the Orange Bowl?

17. Which linebacker holds the school record for most tackles in a season?

18. Who holds the UA record for most interceptions in a career?

19. Who holds the school record for most interceptions in a season?

20. Who holds the Bama record for most tackles in a game?

21. Who set the record for most tackles in a career at UA?

22. Who has the team record for most QB sacks?

23. What do the initials "E.J." stand for in E.J. Junior III's name?

24. Which former UA All-American defensive lineman is now the analyst on New York Jets radio broadcasts?

25. Who is the former Bama defensive back from 1971-74 who is now the head coach at Oregon State?

## What is It?

These diagrams represent six football terms. What are they? Solution on page 152.

1. goal | **STAND**

2. **COVERAGE**
*coverage*

3. BUMP run

4. pas

5. GUARD
→ guard
*GUARD*

6. **BACK**

7. **men on the field men on the field**
**men on the field men on the field**
**men on the field men on the field**
**men on the field men on the field**
**men on the field men on the field**
**men on the field men on the field**

## Short Yardage Crossword

Solution on page 153.

**Across**

1. Pasty-faced
5. Troop 45's cookie selling org.
8. Whodunit board game
9. P from 1977-79, Buddy ___
10. In pain on the field
11. Curved molding
12. Drop the ball
13. Out for the night in the dorm
14. Otherwise (2 wds.)
16. NAPA Auto Parts battery fluid
17. However, informally
20. Distinctive flair
21. UA freshman, probably
22. K from 1968-70, Frank ___
23. Face-to-face exam at UA
24. Bring to bear
25. Sports cable TV award that Mark Ingram got nominated for

**Down**

1. Result of working out too much
2. Cast aspersions on Auburn
3. U. of Miami athlete
4. "Is it soup ___?"
5. Eager beavers
6. Linemen's blocking apparatus
7. Had the wings at Buffalo Phil's
9. Vagabond
13. 1st-___-10
15. *Huckleberry* ___
16. Word of woe
18. Pile
19. The O in SRO
20. Down Under bird
21. Kicker's asset

After solving the crossword puzzle, use the letters in the grid to answer this additional clue. Transfer the letters in numbered boxes to the corresponding blanks below. (Or answer the additional clue first to help you solve the crossword puzzle.)

UA K in 2000-01, Neal ______________

___ ___ ___ ___ ___ ___
17 3 11 22 7 2

## Chapter 8

# Special Teams

While researching the greatest special teams players in Alabama history, one name kept popping up: Tiffin. As in Van Tiffin, the Tide's All-American placekicker from 1983-86, and Leigh Tiffin, the Tide's All-American placekicker from 2006-09.

Van's claims to fame include booting the longest field goal in Bama history (57 yards against Texas A&M in 1985) and making all 135 of his extra point attempts (also a school record). His most memorable kick was a 52-yard field goal as time expired to give UA a 25-23 victory over Auburn in the 1985 Iron Bowl. He spent one season in the NFL (with Miami and Tampa Bay), making 5-of-7 field goals and 11-of-11 extra points. He also fathered Leigh.

Leigh's claims to fame include scoring more points than any person in Alabama history (385), most field goals in a career (83), and most field goals in a season (30). His most memorable kick was a 47-yard game-winning field goal against Vanderbilt. He connected on a long of 54 yards against Clemson in the Chick-fil-A College Kickoff and made four field goals in a game against Mississippi State. He also missed three field goals in a 24-23 overtime loss against Arkansas. Leigh signed with the Cleveland Browns for the 2010 NFL season, but did not play in a game.

Other Bama kickers of note include Philip Doyle (1987-90), Michael Proctor (1992-95), Brian Bostick (2002-04), Ryan Pflugner (1998-99) and Bill Davis (1971-73).

In 2010, Jeremy Shelley (12-of-16 FG, 50-of-51 PAT) and Cade Foster (7-of-9 FG, 7-of-7 PAT) shared kicking chores for the Tide.

The Bama player with the most punts in his career is P.J. Fitzgerald (238 from 2006-08), followed by Chris Mohr (203 from 1985-88). The best career punting average belongs to Greg Gantt (43.6 yards per punt from 1971-73); he's followed by Daniel Pope (43.5 yards from 1995-98) and Malcolm Simmons (42.8 yards from 1981-83).

In 2010, Cody Marshall was UA's punter, averaging 39.2 yards on 41 punts.

As for returners, there's no question that Javier Arenas was the most successful in school history. From 2006-09, he returned seven punts for touchdowns to set an SEC record. He has more punt return yards (1,752) than anyone in Bama history and more kickoff return yards (2,166) than anyone in Bama history, too. He averaged a school record 14.0 yards per punt return in his career and 24.1 yards per kickoff return (6th best in UA history).

"It's great to get records," Arenas said. "Records are something that you can sit back and enjoy when you are old and gray."

Other top punt returners include Harry Gilmer (1944-47), Tony Nathan (1975-78), David Palmer (1991-93), Greg Richardson (1983-86), Gordon Pettus (1945-48) and Willie Shelby (1973-75).

Top kickoff return men at UA were Gilmer, who has the highest career average with 28.7 yards per return, Tyrone Prothro (2003-06), George Ranager (1968-70), Shelby, Gene Jelks (1985-89), Arvin Richard (1997-2000), Bobby Humphrey (1985-88) and Freddie Milons (1998-2001).

The greatest kick blocker in Alabama history was Derrick Thomas, who blocked one field goal and four punts from 1985-88. Leroy Cook (1972-75), Tommy Johnson (1991-94) and Chris James (2001-04) each were credited with four blocked kicks in their careers.

Four times a Bama player has blocked two kicks in a single game: Thomas (in 1988), Terrence Cody (in 2009), Mike Washington (in 1973) and Freddie Pickhard (in 1926).

## Pflugner Sudoku

Here's an 8x8 Sudoku, instead of the standard 9x9. But the rules are the same—use logic to fill in the grid so that every row, column and 2x4 box contains the letters P-F-L-U-G-N-E-R, in honor of Ryan Pflugner. The kicker from Sarasota, Fla., booted a 55-yard field goal against Arkansas in 1998, the second longest in UA history. Solution on page 155.

| | | R | | | | | G |
|---|---|---|---|---|---|---|---|
| | F | | | R | | L | |
| R | | | | F | N | | |
| | | P | G | | | | |
| | | L | E | | | | |
| G | | | | P | E | | |
| | P | | | N | | F | |
| | | F | | | | | U |

## Gilmer Sudoku

Use logic to fill in the grid so every row, column and 2x3 box contains the letters G-I-L-M-E-R, in honor of UA kick returner Harry Gilmer, who led the nation in punt returns in 1945. Solution on page 153.

| | E | | R | G | |
|---|---|---|---|---|---|
| | | L | | | I |
| M | | | L | R | |
| | G | R | | | M |
| E | | | G | | |
| | L | G | | I | |

## Special Teams Crossword

Solution on page 154.

**Across**

1. UA P from 1985-88, Chris ___
5. Nimble, as a kick returner
9. With ___ breath (anxiously)
14. Birmingham Fencing Club weapon
15. UA test choice
16. Martini garnish at Harry's Bar
17. TPD drug buster
18. Some whistle blowers
19. Muscle connector
20. State Liquor Store gin flavor
21. Switch position
22. ADOC death row reprieves
23. California wine valley
25. Aloha Bowl souvenirs
26. UA K from 1971-73, Greg ___
29. Noir's opposite
31. Health resort
34. Like a UA gymnast
35. One way to run
36. ___ Solo of *Star Wars*
37. Full of frills
38. Fly fisherman, often
40. Pothead's pipe
41. Biblical verb ending
42. French father
43. Wooden pin
44. Witness
45. Birmingham Race Course gear
47. UA K from 1987-90, Philip ___
48. 007
49. Light bulb unit
51. What a lenient Tuscaloosa County judge may show
53. BMOC, for one
54. The price to be paid
58. UA calculus class calculation
59. Birmingham Opera star
60. Like many student films
61. Kind of acid
62. Claim
63. Inheriter of the Earth, according to the Bible
64. K Kim or RB Cavan
65. Stone Cold Creamery drink
66. UA P from 1997-98, Daniel ___

**Down**

1. JC Penney department
2. Iridescent gem at Kay Jewelers
3. Momma Goldberg's Deli sandwich
4. Of late
5. Ace Barber Shop sharpener
6. Home built in a day?
7. Dennis the Menace dog
8. "Absolutely!"
9. UA K from 2002-04, Brian ___
10. Assumed name on an Alabama State Police blotter
11. Pint-sized
12. Nights before big games
13. Morning moisture on the field
22. Man of La Mancha
24. Had a pizza at the Crimson Cafe
25. Hobbling, like an injured player
26. Strong winds
27. Playing marble
28. Type of market
30. Weighed down
31. Ostentatious

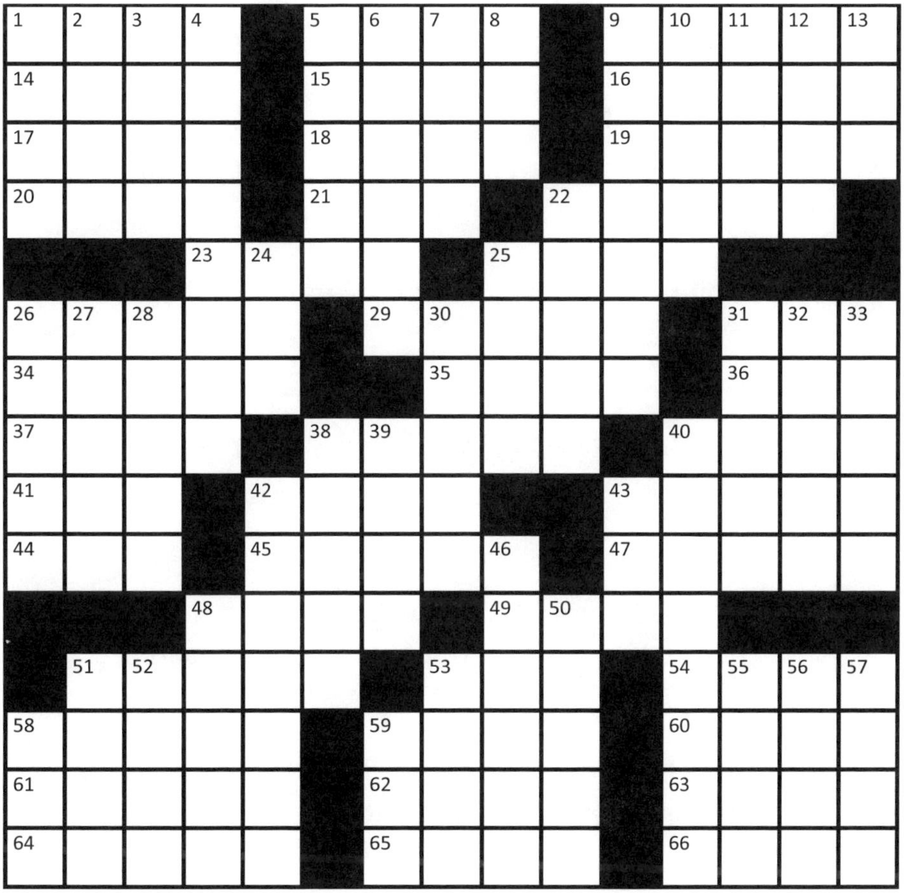

32. Discussion group
33. Central High School geometry calculation
38. Pipsqueak
39. Bone-dry
40. Alabama Guard training center (2 wds.)
42. UA K from 1992-95, Michael ___
43. Banned insecticide
46. Turn
48. Pickling liquid
50. In pieces
51. The silent type
52. Give off, as light
53. Start of a cheer
55. Nabisco cookie
56. Put one's foot down
57. Youngster
58. Once around the track at the UA Recreation Center
59. Guntersville facility

## Special Teams Trivia

Answers on page 153.

1. Who missed the extra point kick in overtime in the 35-34 loss to Michigan in the Orange Bowl on Jan. 1, 2000?

2. What uniform number did kicker Jeremy Shelley wear in 2010?

3. Who was the Tide's kickoff specialist in 2010 who was credited with a fumble forced against Georgia State?

4. True or False? Cody Mandell was a walk-on freshman who won the starting punter spot for the 2010 season.

5. Who was UA's kickoff returner in 2010 who averaged 25.4 yards per return to rank 39th in the nation?

6. Who averaged 8.1 yards on 33 punt returns in 2010 to rank 16th nationally?

7. Which kicker booted six field goals vs. Southwestern Louisiana in 1990?

8. Who kicked the game-winning 45-yard field goal on the final play to give the Tide a 13-10 win over Texas Tech in the 2006 Cotton Bowl?

9. Who kicked a school record 57-yard field goal vs. Texas A&M in 1985?

10. How many 50+ yard field goals did Van Tiffin make from 1983-87?

11. Who made three 50-yard field goals in the 2000 season?

12. Who set the UA season record with 24 field goals in 1990?

13. Who set the UA career scoring record with 345 points from 1987-90?

14. Who broke that career scoring record with 385 points from 2006-08?

15. Who was the freshman walk-on kicker who booted the winning field goal vs. Vanderbilt in 2006?

16. Who did Philip Doyle beat with his final play 47-yard field goal in a 1990 game?

17. Who was the first UA kicker to win an overtime game with a field goal? (Hint: It was 1998 vs. Ole Miss.)

18. Who blocked Penn State's field goal attempt with eight seconds remaining to preserve a 17-16 UA win in 1989?

19. Johnny Cain set a school record in 1932 for most punts in a game. How many did he have?

20. Who finished his career at UA with the highest career punting average?

21. Who set the UA season record (50 or more punts) with a 44.0 yard average in 1998?

22. Dixie Howell set the Bama record for longest punt in 1933. How far was it?

23. Who returned a kickoff 100 yards, tying the school record, against Kentucky in 2004?

24. Who returned a kickoff 96 yards for a touchdown against Auburn in 2003?

25. Who had four blocked punts in 2003?

## Special Teams Word Search

Solution on page 154.

| | | | | | | | | | | | | | | |
|---|---|---|---|---|---|---|---|---|---|---|---|---|---|---|
| E | R | S | A | M | N | E | D | R | A | E | B | A | W | E |
| G | E | A | N | O | S | M | A | I | L | L | I | W | Y | M |
| I | M | N | T | Y | S | T | O | C | K | T | O | N | O | K |
| L | L | E | W | O | H | W | T | H | Z | T | A | H | C | S |
| M | A | R | E | R | M | E | F | A | L | N | R | U | V | H |
| E | P | A | L | L | O | S | V | R | H | A | N | M | N | E |
| R | R | K | Y | E | F | T | D | D | E | G | O | P | E | L |
| P | A | N | O | C | M | R | C | S | I | E | S | H | L | B |
| T | N | I | D | M | A | K | E | O | D | P | L | R | S | Y |
| R | A | F | Q | H | N | C | U | N | R | O | I | E | O | U |
| L | G | F | C | M | N | I | L | Y | G | P | W | Y | N | E |
| I | E | I | O | R | H | T | O | R | P | U | X | P | M | D |
| D | R | T | Y | A | E | S | M | A | I | L | L | I | W | O |
| I | Z | O | A | S | N | O | M | M | I | S | K | F | I | O |
| F | T | N | A | Y | R | B | B | S | U | T | T | E | P | G |

| | | | |
|---|---|---|---|
| ARENAS | GOODE | PETTUS | SEAY |
| BEARDEN | HOWELL | PFLUGNER | SHELBY |
| BOSTICK | HUMPHREY | POPE | SIMMONS |
| BRYANT | KIM | PROCTOR | STOCKTON |
| DIEHL | MANN | PROTHRO | TIFFIN |
| DOYLE | MCELROY | RANAGER | WEST |
| FREELEND | MOHR | RICHARD | WILLIAMS |
| GANTT | NELSON | RICHARDSON | WILLIAMSON |
| GILMER | PALMER | SCHATZ | WILSON |

## Short Yardage Crossword

Solution on page 155.

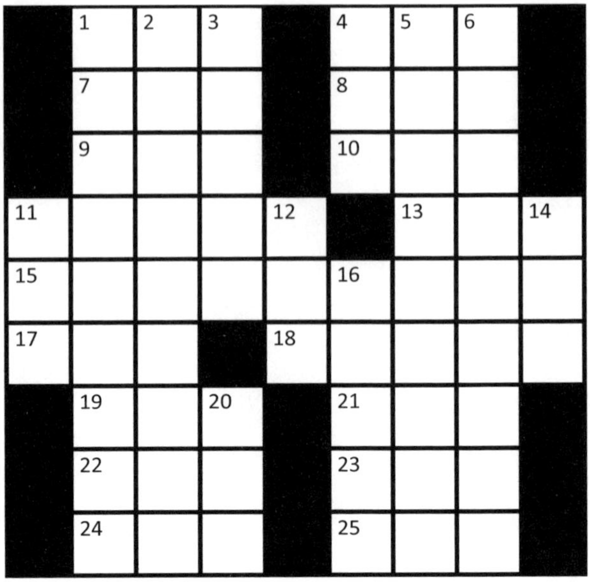

**Across**

1. Little devil
4. Birmingham Zoo beast
7. Female deer
8. Room to watch a Bama game on TV
9. Crimson Tide pitcher's stat
10. Demetrius Hart's uniform number
11. Preface to a UA textbook
13. Bank of Tuscaloosa offering
15. Coach of Bama's 1992 national championship team
17. Wire diameter measure
18. UAB Hospital prescribed amounts
19. Smoke, for short
21. Egyptian boy king
22. Had an egg roll at Lai Lai
23. UA RB, ___ Sharrief
24. Soap ingredient
25. Anatomical pouch

**Down**

1. Indistinguishable, like Ronde and Tiki Barber
2. Fatality rate
3. Necklace item at Reeds Jewelers
4. Commotion
5. Port Angeles, Washington, college
6. Full of pep, like a UA cheerleader
11. Doctrine: Suffix
12. McFarland Plaza store: ___ Navy
14. Beast of burden
16. Itsy-bitsy bits
20. "___ whiz!"

After solving the crossword puzzle, use the letters in the grid to answer this additional clue. Transfer the letters in numbered boxes to the corresponding blanks below. (Or answer the additional clue first to help you solve the crossword puzzle.)

First Tide coach to win 8 games in a season (1919)

___ ___ ___ ___ ___
25 19 12 21 21

## Chapter 9

# Coaches

Paul W. “Bear” Bryant was the head coach of the Crimson Tide for 25 years (1958-82). During that time, Alabama had a 232-46-9 record, won six national championships, captured 13 SEC titles and played in 24 bowl games.

Four weeks after coaching his last game, he died at the age of 69. A memorial outside of Legion Field in Birmingham reads, “If you believe in yourself and have dedication and pride and never quit, you’ll be a winner.”

Bryant was a winner from the time he first began playing organized football as an eighth grader in Fordyce, Ark. Playing on the offensive and defensive lines, he led Fordyce HS to the 1930 state championship. He accepted a scholarship to Alabama and was a starter on the 1934 national championship team. Bryant was selected by the Brooklyn Dodgers in the fourth round of the 1936 NFL Draft. He skipped the pros to begin a coaching career at Union University in Jackson, Tenn. He quickly left Union to return to Bama as an assistant coach under Frank Thomas.

Bryant departed Alabama in 1940 to become an assistant at Vanderbilt. Bryant was offered the head coaching position at the University of Arkansas a year later, but he enlisted in the U.S. Navy instead. After the ship he was on was rammed, he returned to land for the remainder of the war to coach the North Carolina Pre-Flight football team. Following the war, Bryant was hired by the University of Maryland. Maryland was 6-2-1 in 1945 in his only season there.

Bryant moved to Kentucky in 1946 and went 60-23-6 in eight seasons. His 1950 squad was 11-1, won the SEC championship and beat No. 1 ranked Oklahoma in the Sugar Bowl.

In 1954, Bryant was hired by Texas A&M. The Aggies were just 1-9 in Bryant’s first year (the only losing season for Bryant in his 38 years as a head coach), but they improved to 7-2-1 in the second year and won the Southwest Athletic Conference in 1956 while going 9-0-1. The following year, Bryant had Texas A&M in the Top 10 nationally. They finished 8-3 and played in the Gator Bowl. Aggies running back John David Crow won the Heisman Trophy.

Meanwhile, Alabama football was suffering through the worst stretch in school history (a total of four wins in three years). The University had its sights set on bringing Bryant back to Tuscaloosa. It didn't take much to pry him away from Texas A&M. Bryant said, "Momma called. And when Momma calls, you just have to come runnin'."

Bryant's first Tide team in 1959 was 5-4-1. The next season the Tide went 7-2-2 and played in the Liberty Bowl. Bama was 8-1-2 in his third season, then won the national championship in 1961 with an 11-0 record.

When Bryant retired following the 1982 season, he was the winningest coach in the history of college football with 323 wins. He was a three-time national coach of the year (1961, '71 and '73) and the award was eventually named the Paul "Bear" Bryant Award; he was the head coach of *Sports Illustrated*'s NCAA Football All-Century Team; he received the Presidential Medal of Freedom posthumously; Bama's stadium, Bryant-Denny Stadium, is named in his honor; his image was on a U.S. postage stamp in 1996; and Super Bowl XVII was dedicated to him.

So, why was Bryant called "Bear"? Legend has it that as a 13-year-old boy, he wrestled a captive bear during a theater promotion. And why did he wear a houndstooth hat on the sidelines? According to Ken Gaddy of the Paul W. Bryant Museum, Bryant started wearing the hat after winning the 1965 Orange Bowl. That's when New York Jets owner Sonny Werblin offered Bryant the Jets' coaching job. Bryant said no, but the owner sent Bryant a houndstooth hat. When Werblin saw that Bryant was wearing the hat, Werblin continued to send Bryant a new hat every few months.

## Nick Saban Wordsmith Challenge

Using the letters N-I-C-K-S-A-B-A-N, see how many words of four or more letters you can make. We found about 30 fairly common words (plus 49 more not so common ones that are acceptable in a game of SCRABBLE). Proper nouns, foreign words and abbreviations don't count. If you can find 24 or more words in 30 minutes, you're an All-American Wordsmith. Solution on page 156.

## Cryptic Quote

The Cryptic Quote is a substitution cipher in which one letter stands for another. If you think that A equals Z, it will equal Z throughout the puzzle. Solve this Cryptic Quote from Bear Bryant. Solution on page 155.

U Y X X U Z   X N Y D C R

P F W Z   X N Z

E Y S S Z K Z D T Z .

Z H Z K O M D Z   Y R

Q Z U U   I K Z I F K Z E

Y D   X N Z   L Y C

X N Y D C R ,   L V X

M D U O   X N Z

Q Y D D Z K R

I Z K S Z T X

X N Z   U Y X X U Z

X N Y D C R .

## Coaches Trivia

Answers on pag1e 157.

1. Who is the only Auburn grad to serve as a Tide full-time assistant coach? Hint: He's on the staff now.

2. Which school did Bama beat in the 1982 Liberty Bowl in Bear Bryant's last game?

3. True or False? Bear Bryant was selected by the Brooklyn Dodgers in the fourth round of the 1936 NFL Draft.

4. Which college gave Bear Bryant his first heading coaching job?

5. What was the only piece of jewelry Bear Bryant wore?

6. What honor was bestowed posthumously to Bear Bryant by President Ronald Reagan in 1983?

7. Which magazine named Bear Bryant the head coach on its NCAA Football All-Century Team?

8. Who was the defensive coordinator who became the interim head coach for Bama in the 2006 Independence Bowl after Mike Shula was fired?

9. True or False? Mike Shula is the nephew of former NFL coach Don Shula.

10. Who was the first African-American assistant coach at UA?

11. Where was former UA head coach Dennis Franchione named head coach in 2011?

12. Where was Dennis Franchione coaching when he was named head coach at UA in 2001?

13. Which UA head coach was a member of Bama's 1973 national championship team?

14. Who succeeded Bear Bryant as Tide head coach?

15. Who am I?
    * I was on the boards of Tandy Corp. and the Texas Rangers Law Enforcement Assoc.
    * I am a member of the College Football Hall of Fame.
    * I played at Texas A&M from 1954-56 under Bear Bryant.
    * I was head coach at Alabama from 1990-96.

16. Which Bama head coach played 10 years in the NFL for Green Bay (1965-66), Baltimore (1967-72), Houston (1973) and Los Angeles (1974)?

17. Who was Bama's coach before Bear Bryant?

18. Who was UA's head coach when Bear Bryant played?

19. Which UA head football coach also was the school's head baseball coach from 1924-27?

20. Which UA head coach was a teammate of long-time college football and NFL coach Dennis Erickson at Everett (Wash.) High School?

**Nick Saban Trivia**

Answers on page 157.

1. Nick Saban is one of two coaches who has won SEC titles at two schools. Who is the other coach?

2. Which three NFL teams has Saban worked for?

3. Where did he get his first college head coaching job?

4. Which school did Saban's LSU team beat in the BCS Championship Game following the 2003 regular season?

5. Which football movie did Saban have a cameo role, playing himself?

## Coaches Crossword

Solution on page 156.

**Across**

1. Jesse Williams' hairstyle
7. Pale with fright
12. Irrational fear
14. UA postgraduate project
16. Preliminary sketch
17. Go at it on the field
18. "So what ___ is new?"
19. Night watch
21. Dark time for poets
22. Go downhill fast?
25. Back tooth
27. Ready for shipping
30. Lab eggs
31. Some Tuscaloosa City Council votes
35. Cut down
36. Transfer to another school
38. One of two coaches to win an SEC championship at two schools
39. UA baseball pitcher's stat
40. Drink from a dish like an Auburn Tiger?
41. Mythical bird
43. Freudian topic in a UA psych class
44. UA coach who started the Georgia State football program in 2008
46. Football vernacular
48. Patch up a uniform rip
49. Oft injured player's joint
50. Player to TV camera: "Hi, ___!"
51. Some solvents
53. Cut corners
55. BHM posting
56. Cousin of an ostrich
59. Saturate
61. Pro ___
65. Hispanic
67. Run-down dorm rooms
70. SOS lights
71. Levels
72. Tibet's capital
73. Steered steer

**Down**

1. Rough up badly
2. Table scraps
3. Most fit
4. Singer DiFranco
5. Came in first in the SEC
6. Ukraine's capital
7. Number one Hun
8. UA head coach who was named the QB coach of the Carolina Panthers in 2011
9. "For ___ a jolly . . ."
10. Latin 101 verb at UA
11. Cairo's river
12. *The Raven* author
13. Sci-fi writer Isaac
15. Richard Shelby pos.
20. Rule
23. UA coach who had to step down at mid-season due to a case of typhoid fever
24. Brainstorm
26. Genetic inits.
27. UA Chess Club word
28. Air again on WVUA
29. In the know
32. Having a lot to lose?
33. Avid, as a freshman

34. *The* ___ *of Kilimanjaro*
37. Poise
38. UA coach who was a horse racing writer before getting into coaching
42. Curved molding
45. Hi-___ monitor
47. Contaminated
50. Brunch cocktail
52. UA coach who also coached at Ole Miss, ___ Drew
54. UA interim head coach for the 2006 Independence Bowl
56. North Pole toymaker
57. McFarland or University, e.g.
58. 2002 Winter Olympics locale
60. Per person
62. Lotion additive
63. Take care of
64. Beast of burden
66. Bank of Tuscaloosa offering
68. Not just "a"
69. James Taylor hit: ___ *Town Too*

## Who am I? Sudoku

Use logic to fill in the boxes so every row, column and 3x3 box contains the letters in the name of a memorable Alabama coach. (Hint: He was the head coach of Alabama's 1910 team.) When completed, the row indicated by the arrow will spell out his name correctly. Solution on page 156.

| | | | | | | | | | |
|---|---|---|---|---|---|---|---|---|---|
| ▶ | | | | | | | | | |
| | | O | | G | | A | | Y | |
| | | | L | | N | | O | | |
| | | Y | | M | | L | | N | |
| | | | U | | | | A | | |
| | | W | | U | | N | | L | |
| | | | A | | U | | Y | | |
| | | G | | W | | Y | | M | |
| | | | | | | | | | |

## Thomas Sudoku

Use logic to fill in the grid so every row, column and 2x3 box contains the letters T-H-O-M-A-S, in honor of Frank Thomas, the Alabama head coach from 1931-46. Solution on page 155.

| | | | | | |
|---|---|---|---|---|---|
| T | | A | O | | H |
| | | | | | |
| S | | H | A | | |
| | | M | H | | S |
| | | | | | |
| H | | S | M | | T |

*Bear Bryant*

## Short Yardage Crossword

Solution on page 158.

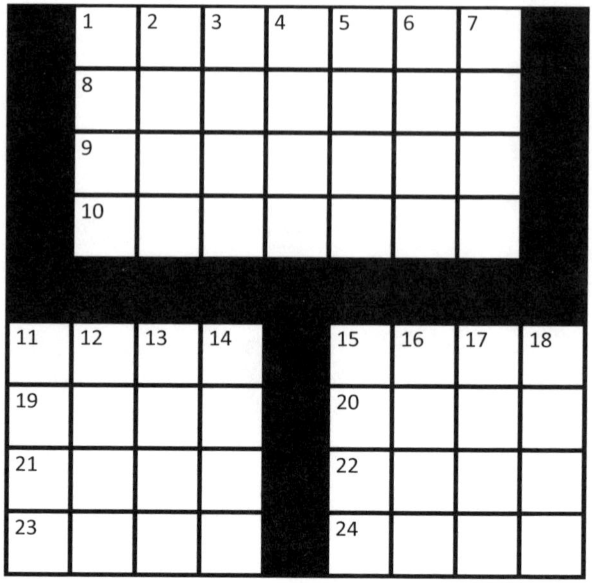


**Across**

1. Moscow native
8. Home of the Champs Sports Bowl
9. Coach Saban's to-do lists
10. Bama's "Ozzie"
11. All-American LB in 1980 and '81
15. 2-time All-American running back in 1931 and '32
19. Truck-full
20. Bygone era of Tide football
21. Poet Pound
22. Mark Prater's winter forecast, maybe
23. Declare untrue in a Tuscaloosa County court
24. Alabama Outdoors shelter

**Down**

1. Horse coloring
2. Encourage
3. Triple Crown winner: Seattle ___
4. ___ souci
5. Prefix with China
6. One who raised Cain
7. Narrow margin of victory
11. Ran, as uniform colors
12. Move slowly
13. Ball material?
14. June 6, 1944
15. Dermatologist's concern
16. Top-of-the-line
17. Caddie's offering at the UA Golf Course
18. Former Speaker Gingrich

After solving the crossword puzzle, use the letters in the grid to answer this additional clue. Transfer the letters in numbered boxes to the corresponding blanks below. (Or answer the additional clue first to help you solve the crossword puzzle.)

UA alum who played Gomer Pyle

___ ___ ___ ___ ___ ___
18 9 11 8 1 22

# Chapter 10

## Overtime

The University of Alabama was founded in 1831 and is the largest school in the state with 30,000 students. The campus was built in Tuscaloosa since the city was the state capital at the time. In 1860, at the dawn of the U.S. Civil War, the University was converted into a military school. Because of that, Union troops burned down the campus in 1865. The school was rebuilt, reopened and reclassified as a public institution without military ties.

Today, the campus is more than 1,000 acres with nearly 300 buildings. It was recently included on a list of the 20 most beautiful colleges in the U.S.

UA was integrated in 1956, but threats of violence caused the school to expel the first African-American student, Autherine Lucy. It wasn't until 1963 that two more African-American students enrolled. That's when Governor George Wallace personally blocked the entrance of Foster Auditorium in an attempt to deny the students access. The federal government intervened, and the students were allowed to attend classes.

The football team plays in Bryant-Denny Stadium on campus. The stadium opened in 1929 and has seen major renovations throughout its existence. The last renovation—in 2010—added seating in the south end zone and upper deck, bringing the stadium capacity to more than 100,000.

The stadium area has a Walk of Champions that includes bronze statues of each Bama football coach who has led UA to a national championship (Wallace Wade, Frank Thomas, Bear Bryant, Gene Stallings and Nick Saban). In addition, pavers on the Walk pay tribute to each national championship and SEC title team. At the North Entrance to the stadium are bronze statues of two players holding a large Alabama flag. One of the players is wearing uniform number 18, the other number 92, to celebrate the year (1892) that the school began playing football.

From 1927 through 2003, the Tide also played "home" games at Birmingham's Legion Field. Bama had a record of 160-52-12 (.741) at Legion Field and a mark of 212-50-3 (.806) at Bryant-Denny Stadium (through the 2010 season).

Why are Alabama sports teams called the Crimson Tide? Originally, the Bama teams were known as the "Varsity" or "Crimson White," referring to the school colors. In 1907, Bama was playing Auburn on a sloppy field in Birmingham that became a sea of red mud. The sports editor of *The Birmingham Age-Herald*, Hugh Roberts, described Bama as the "Crimson Tide" in his game story, and the name stuck.

And why an elephant? Local business owner J.D. Rosenberger outfitted the undefeated 1926 team with "good luck" luggage tags for its trip to the Rose Bowl. Displayed on the tags was his company's logo, a red elephant standing on a trunk. Reporters covering the team saw the tags and compared the players' size to the beasts.

Alabama began play in the Southern Intercollegiate Athletic Association in 1895. Other schools in the original SIAA were Auburn, Georgia, Georgia Tech, North Carolina, Sewanee and Vanderbilt. In 1921, UA and seven other schools left the SIAA over a ban on freshman eligibility and paid summer baseball. UA then became a charter member of the Southern Conference (along with Auburn, Clemson, Georgia, Georgia Tech, Kentucky, Maryland, Mississippi State, North Carolina, North Carolina State, Tennessee, Virginia, Virginia Tech and Washington & Lee). In 1932, UA and 12 other schools of the Southern Conference located west and south of the Appalachian Mountains left and formed the Southeastern Conference. Alabama won its first SEC football championship in 1935 and has remained in the SEC ever since.

## Missing B-A-M-A

Fill in the blanks with the letters B-A-M-A, once each, in any order, to form a fairly common seven-letter word in each line. Solution on page 157.

1. ___ ___ R ___ ___ I D

2. ___ R ___ ___ ___ N D

3. ___ ___ C ___ ___ R E

4. L ___ ___ ___ ___ S T

5. ___ ___ N T ___ ___ S

6. ___ ___ T H ___ ___ T

7. ___ ___ I ___ ___ L E

8. ___ O ___ T ___ ___ N

9. ___ ___ I L ___ ___ G

10. ___ ___ Y S ___ ___ L

## Overtime Crossword

Solution on page 159.

**Across**

1. Animated graphics in a movie at the Alabama International Film Festival, briefly
4. Modernize Bama's football media guide
10. Light on one's feet, as a kick returner
14. Hasty escape from the Tuscaloosa County Jail
15. Verner Elementary School playground equipment
16. It follows New and Good in an Alabama atlas
17. Sphere seen from the Children's Hands-On Museum planetarium
18. Stir up the campus housing units and anagram of CRIMSON TIDE (2 wds.)
20. Part of TCCU
22. "Frequently," at the Slash Pine Poetry Festival
23. "Are we there ___?"
24. Remove errors from
25. Alabama State Mineral: red iron ___
27. Have the fried green tomatoes at The Cypress Inn
30. Leave in, to an editor at *The Crimson White*
31. Starbucks drink topped with marshmallows
34. Not tricked by the opposing team
35. Hole-making tool
37. West Alabama Humane Society's frisky feline
39. Unimportant orders from the head coach and anagram of CRIMSON TIDE (2 wds.)
41. North River Yacht Club sundial indicator
43. 1990s coupe at Tuscaloosa Toyota
44. Punts' paths
45. "A merry heart ___ good like a medicine": Proverbs
47. Companion of mean and median in a UA statistics class
51. Alabama's Civil War side: Abbr.
52. Football air pressure meas.
53. Exchange vows at Chapel In The Pines
54. Locklear Kia model
56. Grazing locale
59. Bama Art House Film Series flick, often
60. X-rated campus intellects and anagram of CRIMSON TIDE (2 wds.)
64. Moore Facility building addition
65. Locks in a Birmingham Race Course barn
66. Like hair, usually, after combing
67. Former Tide DB, ___ Sharrief
68. Use the Don Gambril Olympic Pool
69. World Heritage List maintainer: Abbr.
70. It was dropped on campus in the '60s

**Down**

1. Sun blockers
2. Andre Smith's January birthstone
3. Drink at the Houndstooth
4. Taking advantage of
5. Instrument for signing a National Letter of Intent
6. Denny Chimes tower design: art ___
7. "Beat Bama? In your dreams!" (2 wds.)
8. Player's body art
9. Alabama State Fair barn female
10. Sneaker, e.g.
11. Omens
12. Talladega Superspeedway dashboard abbr.
13. Obama campaign slogan: ___ We Can
19. Turn crimson, perhaps
21. Beats at Southeast Auction Company

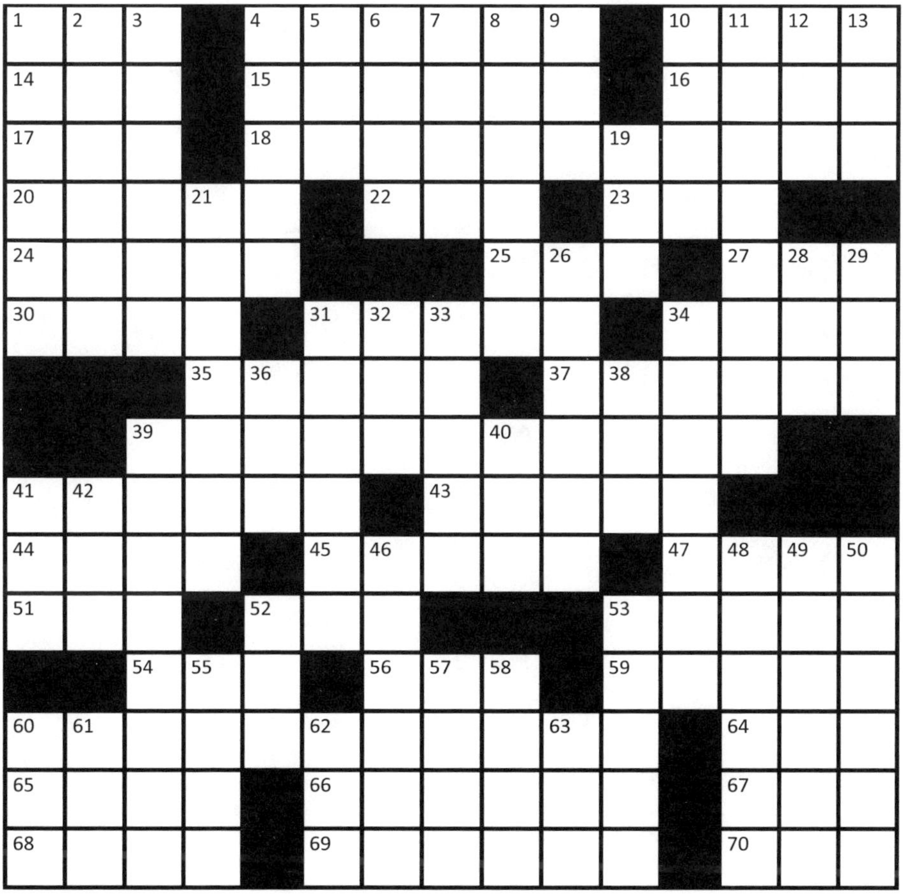

26. Debonair, like Coach Bryant
28. Had a burger at Jack's
29. Weight of the entire offensive line
31. Bryant-Denny Stadium throngs
32. *Star-Spangled Banner* preposition
33. Thin pancake at the Tuscaloosa IHOP
34. Place to put up one's feet while watching a game on TV
36. Lennon's love
38. Treatment for a player's sprained ankle
39. Logan's Roadhouse specialty: ___ and cheese
40. Not dis
41. Cul-de-___
42. Redbox rental: *48* ___
46. Many a wealthy Longhorns fan
48. Trying experience
49. Football practice activities
50. Site for lashes
52. Aloha Bowl dish
53. Botch, like running the wrong pass pattern
55. News bit in *The Tuscaloosa News*
57. Leprechaun's land
58. West End Park picnic pests
60. Pat Trammell pair?
61. Inexperienced, like a freshman player
62. PC "brain"
63. Blue-Gray Football Classic mo.

## One and Only One

Alabama wears uniforms designed by Nike. Hidden in the grid is one and only one complete NIKE. See if you can find it. Solution on page 159.

N K I E I N N K E I N I K I N
I K E N K I E N I K K I N E I
K E I N I E K I I K N I K N K
N I K K E I N K K E N E K N I
N I K K N N I K I N K I N K E
I K E N I K I K E N I K K E I
N K I E E E K K K I I I N N N
I N K E N K K I I N I I K I I
K I I N K E N K I E K N E K N
I N K E K I K E E E K I E I E
N E K E K K I E E N K I I K N
I E K K E N N E I I K E K I K
K N I N N E N N E N I N I E I
N E K I I N K E I N N K E N I
I N I E I K E I K E I N K I N

## Find the Words

Starting anywhere in the box, use adjacent letters—vertically, horizontally or diagonally—to make as many words as you can from the letters in ROLL TIDE ROLL BAMA. Words need to be four or more letters and cannot use the same letter cube more than once per word. No proper nouns, hyphenated or foreign words and no slang. We found about 60 common words, but there are a total of 206 words that are in *The Official SCRABBLE Players Dictionary*. Find 50 words in 60 minutes to earn induction into the Solving Hall of Fame. List of words on page 158.

| | | | |
|---|---|---|---|
| R | O | L | L |
| T | I | D | E |
| R | O | L | L |
| B | A | M | A |

## Tide TXT

Use your cell phone keypad to help decode the last names of these Alabama players. In the example 2639, the 2 could be A, B or C; the 6 could be M, N or O; the 3 could be D, E or F; and the 9 could be W, X, Y or Z. The player's name found in that text is C-O-D-Y, Terrence Cody, the All-American nose guard in 2008 and '09. Now try these. Answers on page 157.

1. 227537
2. 5646766
3. 846627
4. 464726
5. 79267
6. 7762867
7. 2366388
8. 6225246

## Across & Down Words

There are 11 football terms and a UA football phrase in the diagram. Taking one letter from each box across the top row, find a 4-letter football term. Cross off the letters as you use them. Do the same for the other six rows. Then take one of the remaining letters from each box and go down the first column to find a 7-letter football term. Cross off those letters. Do the same for the other three columns. The remaining letters, one per box, will reveal the phrase, reading left to right, row by row. Solution on page 157.

### Across Words

| | | | |
|---|---|---|---|
| R<br>S T | O<br>Q U | D<br>S U | H<br>K T |
| A<br>P H | A<br>E U | A<br>E S | I<br>S S |
| C<br>P T | A<br>E L | A<br>F R | C<br>N Y |
| C<br>K P | O<br>R U | E<br>N N | F<br>K T |
| B<br>E L | A<br>R T | E<br>L N | L<br>N O |
| E<br>C F | E<br>E L | A<br>C S | F<br>G H |
| A<br>D E | M<br>N R | D<br>E P | F<br>S S |

### Down Words

**Hidden Phrase** ______________________________

## Roll Tide Categories

For each of the categories listed, come up with a word or phrase beginning with each letter of the words ROLL TIDE. Our solution on page 158.

| | UA Offensive Player Past or Present | UA Defensive Player Past or Present |
|---|---|---|
| R | | |
| O | | |
| L | | |
| L | | |
| T | | |
| I | | |
| D | | |
| E | | |

| | Football Term | Alabama City |
|---|---|---|
| R | | |
| O | | |
| L | | |
| L | | |
| T | | |
| I | | |
| D | | |
| E | | |

## Overtime Trivia

Answers on page 160.

1. Which former UA coach wrote, *Another Season: A Coach's Story of Raising an Exceptional Son,* about his son who was born with Down syndrome?

2. Who was the UA quarterback from 1917-19 who is a member of the Baseball Hall of Fame?

3. Name the Bama halfback who was MVP of the 1926 Rose Bowl, then posed for the cover of a Wheaties box and appeared in more than 150 movies from 1927-66.

4. What is Bama's longest winning streak in the *Third Saturday in October* rivalry?

5. What is the name of the trophy awarded to the winning team in the Iron Bowl?

6. What is UA's marching band called?

7. Who is the SEC commissioner?

8. What was the name of the fictional Alabama football player in the book-made-into-a-movie written by Winston Groom?

9. Who played the Bear in the movie *The Bear*?

10. Who played the Bear in the stage play *Bear Country*?

11. Which former UA player wrote the children's book *Roll Tide!*?

12. Which former UA player was an analyst on *Monday Night Football* broadcasts?

13. For the 2006 Ole Miss game, UA players wore special trim around the collars of their uniforms. What was it?

14. Who is the Denny of Bryant-Denny Stadium?

15. When was the first game played in Bryant-Denny Stadium?

16. Bear Bryant had a 72-2 lifetime record at Bryant-Denny Stadium. Which schools did he lose to?

17. What was significant about UA's game on Sept. 27, 1940, against Spring Hill College at Mobile?

18. What was significant about UA's game on Oct. 20, 1951, against Tennessee at Birmingham?

19. Of the schools Bama has played at least five times, which has the best all-time W-L record against UA?

20. Which school is UA 20-0-1 against all-time?

21. What is the Capstone Creed?

22. Who is UA's president?

23. What is the name on the campus chimes, a campanile equipped with a 25-bell carillon, on the Quad?

24. Who is the Voice of UA Football?

25. Which of these men did NOT attend UA: Mel Allen, Jimmy Carter, Bernie Madoff or Latrell Sprewell?

## Nesbit Sudoku

Use logic to fill in the grid so every row, column and 2x3 box contains the letters N-E-S-B-I-T, in honor of James Nesbit, an All-American fullback for Alabama in 1936. Solution on page 158.

| | B | | | | |
|---|---|---|---|---|---|
| | | T | N | | |
| | | B | E | | T |
| I | | E | S | | |
| | | N | I | | |
| | | | | S | |

*Don Hutson*

# Answers

## Chapter 1

### Short Yardage Crossword (from page 4)

Additional Clue Answer: PERKINS

| W | E | B | B | ■ | ■ | C | H | I |
|---|---|---|---|---|---|---|---|---|
| O | V | E | R | S | ■ | O | A | R |
| K | E | N | Y | A | ■ | D | N | A |
| ■ | S | T | A | B | B | E | D | ■ |
| ■ | ■ | ■ | N | B | A | ■ | ■ | ■ |
| ■ | R | E | T | A | R | D | S | ■ |
| C | A | R | ■ | T | R | E | A | D |
| P | S | I | ■ | H | O | L | L | Y |
| A | T | E | ■ | ■ | N | I | K | E |

### Ingram Sudoku (from page 7)

| A | I | G | M | N | R |
|---|---|---|---|---|---|
| M | R | N | I | A | G |
| G | A | R | N | I | M |
| N | M | I | G | R | A |
| R | N | M | A | G | I |
| I | G | A | R | M | N |

### Who Am I? Sudoku (from page 7)

Derrick SLAUGHTER

| | | | | | | | | | |
|---|---|---|---|---|---|---|---|---|---|
| | R | U | E | A | T | L | G | S | H |
| | L | A | G | R | H | S | U | T | E |
| | H | T | S | G | E | U | A | R | L |
| | U | E | R | T | L | A | S | H | G |
| ► | S | L | A | U | G | H | T | E | R |
| | G | H | T | S | R | E | L | A | U |
| | E | G | U | H | A | T | R | L | S |
| | A | R | L | E | S | G | H | U | T |
| | T | S | H | L | U | R | E | G | A |

## History Crossword (from page 10)

| | | | | | | | | | | | | | | |
|---|---|---|---|---|---|---|---|---|---|---|---|---|---|---|
| H | A | L | L | | R | U | D | D | | D | A | R | B | Y |
| O | R | E | O | | U | S | E | R | | A | D | O | R | E |
| R | E | A | R | | T | U | B | E | | I | D | E | A | S |
| N | A | K | E | D | | A | T | W | I | L | L | | | |
| | | | | N | I | L | | | N | I | E | C | E | S |
| J | O | R | D | A | N | | M | A | N | E | | A | A | H |
| A | R | I | A | | C | L | O | P | | S | I | N | G | E |
| Z | I | O | N | | H | O | T | E | L | | M | O | L | E |
| Z | E | T | A | S | | B | O | X | Y | | A | L | E | S |
| E | N | E | | P | E | E | R | | N | A | M | A | T | H |
| S | T | R | E | E | T | | | P | N | C | | | | |
| | | | I | N | C | I | T | E | | E | M | O | T | E |
| H | E | A | D | S | | A | R | A | B | | A | H | O | Y |
| R | A | N | E | E | | M | E | R | E | | R | I | L | E |
| S | T | A | R | R | | B | E | L | L | | T | O | D | D |

## Bama Hodgepodge (from page 8)

All-Americans: CODY, COOK, HAND, LOWE, LYONS, RYANS; Coaches: BRYANT, DUBOSE, PERKINS, SABAN, SHULA; Bowl Games: GATOR, ROSE, SUN, SUGAR; Rivals: AUBURN, LSU, TENNESSEE; Colors: CRIMSON, WHITE; Athletic Director: MOORE.

Hidden Phrase: YEA, ALABAMA! DROWN 'EM TIDE! EVERY 'BAMA MAN'S BEHIND YOU; HIT YOUR STRIDE! (The first lines of the chorus of the fight song, *Yea, Alabama!*)

## History Trivia (from page 13)

1. Linebackers Woodrow Lowe (1973-75) and Cornelius Bennett (1984-86).
2. Antonio Langham.
3. 28.
4. Southern Cal, 21-20. Bama was ranked seventh at the time.
5. 1936; the Tide finished fourth.
6. 1961.
7. 25 wins and no losses.
8. Tennessee.
9. That was the first year that the players' names were put on the back of the game jerseys.
10. Wallace Wade, Frank Thomas, Bear Bryant and Gene Stallings.
11. Colorado.
12. Derrick Thomas (1988) and Rolando McClain (2009).
13. Harry Gilmer (1944-47), Pooley Hubert (1922-25) and Riley Smith (1934-35).
14. John Hannah, Woodrow Lowe, Johnny Musso and Ozzie Newsome.
15. John Hannah.
16. Big Al.
17. Grass.
18. 2003; Alabama beat South Florida, 40-17.
19. Hey (insert opposing school's name)!
    Hey (insert opposing school's name)!
    Hey (insert opposing school's name)!
    We just beat the hell out of you!
    Rammer Jammer, Yellowhammer, give 'em hell, Alabama!
20. Faithful, loyal, firm and true,
    Heart bound to heart will beat
    Year by year, the ages through
    Until in Heaven we meet.
21. 101,821.
22. Lee Roy Jordan.
23. Joe Namath.
24. Ozzie Newsome.
25. Dixie Howell, Cisco Mancha, The Italian Stallion Musso, General Smith.

# Chapter 2

## Word Builder (from page 21)

1. EAR; 2. BYE; 3. KEY; 4. REB; 5. RYE; 6. AREA; 7. YEAR; 8. BEAR; 9. RARE; 10. BERRY; 11. BRAKE; 12. RAKER; 13. BAKERY; 14. JAY BARKER.

## Bryant Pop Up Quote (from page 27)

"LOSING DOES NOT MAKE ME WANT TO QUIT. IT MAKES ME WANT TO FIGHT HARDER."

**Short Yardage Crossword (from page 16)**

Additional Clue Answer: ARENAS

| | P | A | R | | S | A | M | |
|---|---|---|---|---|---|---|---|---|
| | R | N | A | | C | P | U | |
| | O | C | T | | A | P | R | |
| N | T | H | | S | L | O | A | N |
| B | R | O | T | H | E | R | L | Y |
| C | U | R | R | Y | | T | I | C |
| | D | A | Y | | S | I | S | |
| | E | G | O | | H | O | T | |
| | S | E | N | | E | N | S | |

**Jordan Sudoku (from page 19)**

| J | O | D | N | R | A |
|---|---|---|---|---|---|
| N | R | A | J | O | D |
| A | D | R | O | N | J |
| O | N | J | A | D | R |
| D | J | O | R | A | N |
| R | A | N | D | J | O |

**Championship Teams Word Search (from page 20)**

| G | Y | Q | R | E | B | U | H | B | A | R | R | O | N | R |
|---|---|---|---|---|---|---|---|---|---|---|---|---|---|---|
| H | V | V | I | Z | F | L | N | O | S | N | H | O | J | O |
| M | A | R | G | N | I | A | L | C | C | M | T | Y | P | G |
| N | I | F | F | I | T | I | Z | A | T | G | M | A | Z | E |
| S | N | K | Y | Y | Z | D | R | G | N | I | K | J | N | R |
| I | O | U | C | J | G | P | W | I | L | L | I | A | M | S |
| V | M | H | O | I | E | W | H | C | R | U | H | C | P | U |
| A | C | N | C | N | R | S | A | N | E | R | A | K | R | E |
| D | E | T | T | A | A | E | H | H | A | N | K | S | E | R |
| S | L | E | Z | W | L | C | D | A | S | N | C | O | A | A |
| G | R | E | E | N | D | V | T | A | R | P | D | N | M | D |
| C | O | H | I | G | H | T | O | W | E | R | U | E | E | P |
| O | Y | L | L | A | D | O | O | W | E | D | I | K | R | K |
| D | Y | H | V | M | C | C | O | Y | E | L | L | E | M | S |
| Y | K | E | E | P | P | C | J | O | R | D | A | N | F | H |

**Bama Holes (from page 31)**

NATIONAL CHAMPIONS

## Neighbors Sudoku (from page 19)

| R | E | G | B | N | I | O | H | S |
|---|---|---|---|---|---|---|---|---|
| H | O | I | E | S | R | N | G | B |
| B | N | S | G | H | O | E | R | I |
| G | R | N | H | I | B | S | E | O |
| I | S | H | N | O | E | G | B | R |
| O | B | E | S | R | G | H | I | N |
| S | I | O | R | G | H | B | N | E |
| E | G | R | O | B | N | I | S | H |
| N | H | B | I | E | S | R | O | G |

## Knight Moves, Parts I and II (from pages 30)

| 18 | 59 | 50 | 1 | 48 | 15 | 22 | 63 |
|---|---|---|---|---|---|---|---|
| 51 | 2 | 17 | 60 | 21 | 64 | 47 | 14 |
| 58 | 19 | 4 | 49 | 16 | 23 | 62 | 45 |
| 3 | 52 | 57 | 20 | 61 | 46 | 13 | 24 |
| 34 | 5 | 40 | 53 | 36 | 25 | 44 | 11 |
| 39 | 56 | 35 | 8 | 41 | 12 | 29 | 26 |
| 6 | 33 | 54 | 37 | 28 | 31 | 10 | 43 |
| 55 | 38 | 7 | 32 | 9 | 42 | 27 | 30 |

## Championship Teams Trivia (from page 24)

1. Freddie Milons.
2. Marcell Dareus (who also returned an interception for a touchdown just before halftime).
3. Tyrone King.
4. Florida, 28-21.
5. Miami (Fla.), 34-13, which entered the game ranked No. 1.
6. Derrick Lassic.
7. 1979.

8. Ohio State, but the Buckeyes lost to Southern Cal, 17-16, in the Rose Bowl.
9. To No. 7 Southern Cal, 24-14, in Week 3.
10. Notre Dame, 24-23.
11. Ken Stabler, who led Bama to an 11-0 record in 1966 and an 8-2-1 mark in '67 as the starter.
12. Fifth ranked Texas, 21-17.
13. Defensive tackle Billy Neighbors.
14. True; Texas A&M had 11 turnovers.
15. Wallace Wade.
16. Frank Thomas.
17. Penn State, 14-7.
18. Johnny Cain.
19. Frank Howard.
20. Paul Bryant.
21. Mark Ingram.
22. Dr Pepper.
23. Tony Nathan.
24. Pop Warner.
25. Legion Field in Birmingham.

**Championship Teams Crossword (from page 22)**

| M | A | K | E | | K | R | I | S | | B | R | A | S | H |
|---|---|---|---|---|---|---|---|---|---|---|---|---|---|---|
| O | G | R | E | | H | E | R | E | | R | O | P | E | R |
| R | E | A | L | | A | L | O | E | | Y | A | R | N | S |
| G | N | U | S | | K | E | N | | W | A | D | | | |
| A | D | S | | S | I | N | | W | O | N | | C | H | I |
| N | A | S | A | L | | T | A | R | O | T | | L | O | T |
| | | | D | U | E | | R | E | D | | T | A | P | S |
| | C | H | A | M | P | I | O | N | S | H | I | P | S | |
| P | R | I | M | | I | S | M | | Y | E | T | | | |
| R | E | V | | I | L | I | A | D | | R | O | T | O | R |
| O | W | E | | N | O | S | | U | F | O | | E | N | E |
| | | | E | G | G | | S | P | A | | M | A | L | I |
| S | O | L | A | R | | B | A | L | I | | A | G | I | N |
| O | P | E | R | A | | A | V | E | R | | T | U | N | E |
| P | S | A | L | M | | S | E | X | Y | | H | E | E | D |

# Chapter 3

### Short Yardage Crossword (from page 32)

Additional Clue Answer: BARNES

| | | | | | | | | |
|---|---|---|---|---|---|---|---|---|
| C | R | O | Y | L | E | ■ | ■ | ■ |
| S | E | N | I | O | R | I | T | Y |
| A | I | R | P | L | A | N | E | S |
| ■ | ■ | E | E | L | ■ | D | R | E |
| M | A | C | ■ | ■ | ■ | I | R | R |
| M | A | O | ■ | N | I | A | ■ | ■ |
| C | A | R | N | A | T | I | O | N |
| M | A | D | E | S | E | N | S | E |
| ■ | ■ | ■ | B | A | R | K | E | R |

### Croyle Sudoku (from page 35)

| | | | | | |
|---|---|---|---|---|---|
| R | C | L | E | O | Y |
| E | Y | O | L | C | R |
| C | L | Y | O | R | E |
| O | R | E | Y | L | C |
| L | E | C | R | Y | O |
| Y | O | R | C | E | L |

### Quarterbacks Crossword (from page 42)

| | | | | | | | | | | | | | | |
|---|---|---|---|---|---|---|---|---|---|---|---|---|---|---|
| P | I | N | A | T | A | ■ | E | S | P | Y | ■ | A | C | T |
| I | R | O | N | I | C | ■ | T | H | R | O | ■ | L | A | O |
| N | A | M | A | T | H | ■ | H | A | I | R | ■ | A | R | K |
| ■ | ■ | ■ | ■ | L | E | I | ■ | M | C | E | L | R | O | Y |
| S | T | A | V | E | ■ | G | L | E | E | ■ | A | M | M | O |
| H | O | S | E | ■ | F | L | U | ■ | D | E | B | ■ | ■ | ■ |
| U | N | I | T | ■ | I | O | N | S | ■ | A | S | K | E | W |
| L | E | D | ■ | G | R | O | A | N | E | R | ■ | A | L | A |
| A | R | E | N | A | ■ | S | T | A | R | ■ | A | L | O | T |
| ■ | ■ | ■ | U | S | E | ■ | I | C | E | ■ | D | E | P | T |
| P | A | L | M | ■ | Y | U | C | K | ■ | P | O | S | E | S |
| S | T | A | B | L | E | R | ■ | S | P | A | ■ | ■ | ■ | ■ |
| A | T | M | ■ | A | L | G | A | ■ | H | U | N | T | E | R |
| L | A | P | ■ | M | I | E | N | ■ | E | L | A | I | N | E |
| M | R | S | ■ | E | D | D | Y | ■ | W | I | N | C | E | D |

### Crossing Patterns (from page 38)

1. JAY BARKER; 2. DAVID SMITH; 3. ANDREW ZOW; 4. WALTER LEWIS; 5. SCOTT HUNTER; 6. BART STARR.

### Pick a Letter (from page 36)

1. CROYLE; 2. WATTS; 3. SHULA; 4. KITCHENS; 5. WOODSON; 6. DAVIS; 7. STABLER; 8. NAMATH; 9. TRAMMEL; 10. RUTLEDGE.

## Mike Shula Sudoku (from page 35)

| I | M | H | L | K | U | A | E | S |
|---|---|---|---|---|---|---|---|---|
| L | E | U | M | S | A | I | K | H |
| K | S | A | I | E | H | L | M | U |
| M | H | K | S | A | I | E | U | L |
| E | U | I | H | L | M | S | A | K |
| S | A | L | E | U | K | M | H | I |
| A | I | E | K | H | S | U | L | M |
| H | L | M | U | I | E | K | S | A |
| U | K | S | A | M | L | H | I | E |

## Quarterbacks Word Search (from page 37)

| X | W | B | Z | J | J | P | S | N | A | M | A | T | H | H |
|---|---|---|---|---|---|---|---|---|---|---|---|---|---|---|
| L | E | A | R | R | A | T | S | N | E | H | C | T | I | K |
| L | M | R | W | R | S | H | F | H | Z | N | R | Y | S | D |
| E | B | N | K | N | W | R | Q | O | O | O | O | J | L | A |
| M | C | E | L | R | O | Y | L | B | W | S | Y | L | O | V |
| M | R | S | M | D | R | T | K | S | I | K | L | E | A | I |
| A | X | N | G | E | G | N | G | O | T | C | E | W | N | S |
| R | M | R | T | G | L | N | O | N | P | A | A | I | O | K |
| T | U | N | J | I | I | A | Y | S | I | J | B | S | S | R |
| B | U | T | Y | L | K | D | S | O | D | N | B | L | L | E |
| H | O | P | L | M | C | C | A | R | R | O | N | C | E | K |
| T | E | O | A | E | D | U | N | N | C | T | O | E | N | R |
| I | H | B | E | R | D | A | W | A | T | T | S | W | P | A |
| M | N | J | H | K | O | G | J | A | L | U | H | S | C | B |
| S | W | F | S | A | T | M | E | M | O | S | L | E | Y | C |

## Quarterbacks Trivia (from page 39)

1. Ed Salem.
2. Steadman Shealy.
3. Terry Davis.
4. One B.
5. 14, vs. Florida International.
6. Scott Hunter.
7. John Parker Wilson, who had 2,950 total yards in 2007.

8. Gary Hollingsworth at Mississippi on Nov. 4, 1989.
9. Freddie Kitchens.
10. Jay Barker at 35-2-1 from 1991-94, but with forfeits, he was 26-11-1.
11. Pat Trammell.
12. Pat Trammell.
13. Jeff Rutledge.
14. Brodie Croyle.
15. Andrew Zow.
16. Brian Burgdorf.
17. Walter Lewis.
18. Richard Todd.
19. Richard Todd.
20. Gary Rutledge.
21. Ken Stabler.
22. Joe Namath.
23. Joe Namath.
24. Punting average.
25. Tyler Watts.

### QB Quote Box (from page 36)

FIDDLER ON THE ROOF

| 7 | 6 | 5 | 16 |
|---|---|---|---|
| 8 | 1 | 4 | 15 |
| 9 | 2 | 3 | 14 |
| 10 | 11 | 12 | 13 |

## Chapter 4

### What's in a Name? (from page 47)

1. KENNETH DARBY; 2. MARK INGRAM; 3. CHRIS ANDERSON; 4. ED MORGAN; 5. CORKY THARP; 6. PAUL CARRUTH; 7. DERRICK LASSIC; 8. WILBUR JACKSON; 9. RICKY MOORE; 10. SIRAN STACY. RUSS CRAFT = TURF SCARS.

### Double Switch (from page 51)

1. KENNETH DARBY; 2. AHMAAD GALLOWAY; 3. SHAUN ALEXANDER; 4. DENNIS RIDDLE; 5. SIRAN STACY; 6. RICKY MOORE; 7. BILLY JACKSON; 8. TONY NATHAN; 9. CALVIN CULLIVER; 10. ED MORGAN.

### Ifs and Thens (from page 56)

HUMPHREY.

**Short Yardage Crossword (from page 44)**

Additional Clue Answer: BRAGGS

| | | | | | | | | |
|---|---|---|---|---|---|---|---|---|
| | | | R | A | G | | | |
| | | B | E | L | O | W | | |
| | C | O | M | E | D | I | C | |
| H | E | L | I | X | | N | O | W |
| A | L | E | X | A | N | D | E | R |
| P | E | R | | N | E | E | D | Y |
| | B | O | R | D | E | R | S | |
| | | S | E | E | D | S | | |
| | | | M | R | S | | | |

**Suther Sudoku (from page 50)**

| | | | | | |
|---|---|---|---|---|---|
| R | H | U | T | E | S |
| T | E | S | R | H | U |
| U | R | H | S | T | E |
| S | T | E | H | U | R |
| E | S | T | U | R | H |
| H | U | R | E | S | T |

**Running Backs Crossword (from page 48)**

| | | | | | | | | | | | | | | |
|---|---|---|---|---|---|---|---|---|---|---|---|---|---|---|
| M | U | S | S | O | | M | O | O | R | E | | W | H | O |
| O | N | T | A | P | | A | V | I | A | N | | I | O | N |
| O | F | A | G | E | | Y | A | L | T | A | | L | E | E |
| E | R | R | | D | R | A | T | | E | T | A | L | | |
| D | E | E | P | | E | N | I | D | | E | L | I | T | E |
| | E | R | I | C | A | | O | U | R | | P | A | I | L |
| | | | E | L | D | | N | A | I | L | | M | R | S |
| B | A | H | R | A | I | N | | L | O | O | K | S | E | E |
| E | M | U | | P | L | E | A | | T | I | E | | | |
| E | M | M | Y | | Y | A | M | | A | N | G | E | R | |
| R | O | P | E | D | | T | A | L | C | | S | L | E | W |
| | | H | A | W | S | | T | U | T | S | | O | V | A |
| S | I | R | | E | A | G | E | R | | C | A | P | E | R |
| A | L | E | | E | N | S | U | E | | A | L | E | R | T |
| P | L | Y | | B | E | A | R | D | | D | A | R | B | Y |

**Running Backs Trivia (from page 52)**

1. Siran Stacy.
2. On Sept. 16, 2008, he was sentenced to seven years in prison for money laundering and fraud.
3. Stanford's Toby Gerhart. Ingram had 1,304 points, Gerhart 1,276.
4. Matt Leinart of Southern Cal in 2004.

5. Glen Coffee, who had 1,417 yards and 10 TDs.
6. Kenneth Darby.
7. Texas Tech, but he transferred to Alabama.
8. To honor his high school teammate, Mario Reed, who suffered a severe spinal cord injury in a game.
9. Shaun Alexander.
10. Mike Fracchia.
11. Johnny Musso.
12. Shaun Alexander.
13. Wilbur Jackson, 7.2 yards per carry from 1971-73.
14. Chris Anderson.
15. Bobby Humphrey.
16. Harry Gilmer.
17. Harry Gilmer.
18. Gene Jelks.
19. Ricky Moore.
20. Johnny Davis.
21. Calvin Culliver in 1973 and '74.
22. Running back Wilbur Jackson who said, "I just wanted to go to college, get an education, and play football. I didn't want to be Jackie Robinson."
23. Steve Bisceglia.
24. Thomas Allen Tharp.
25. Bobby Marlow.

## Running Backs Word Search (from page 57)

| S | L | L | A | W | T | F | A | R | C | X | N | P | Y | L |
|---|---|---|---|---|---|---|---|---|---|---|---|---|---|---|
| A | W | M | A | R | L | O | W | S | H | D | A | R | B | Y |
| L | I | K | F | O | N | M | M | G | H | R | H | A | Q | A |
| E | L | D | F | N | I | A | U | H | W | E | T | H | D | G |
| X | L | T | T | N | V | R | S | T | C | C | A | T | O | J |
| A | I | L | B | O | L | G | S | U | O | N | N | L | A | E |
| N | A | H | I | S | A | N | O | R | M | E | O | C | Y | L |
| D | M | U | S | R | C | I | A | R | S | P | K | I | C | K |
| E | S | M | C | E | P | Q | H | A | T | S | G | S | A | S |
| R | I | P | E | D | E | S | E | C | O | I | N | S | T | H |
| I | V | H | G | N | J | H | R | N | C | J | A | A | S | O |
| D | A | R | L | A | I | I | R | E | K | A | G | L | F | L |
| D | D | E | I | C | U | L | L | I | V | E | R | O | O | M |
| L | A | Y | A | W | O | L | L | A | G | G | O | F | S | X |
| E | W | O | A | N | E | L | S | O | N | A | M | W | O | B |

**Tom Calvin Sudoku (from page 50)**

| C | T | I | O | A | N | M | L | V |
|---|---|---|---|---|---|---|---|---|
| N | V | A | L | M | T | O | I | C |
| L | M | O | C | I | V | N | A | T |
| M | O | L | V | N | A | T | C | I |
| V | I | N | T | L | C | A | O | M |
| A | C | T | M | O | I | L | V | N |
| T | L | M | I | C | O | V | N | A |
| O | A | C | N | V | M | I | T | L |
| I | N | V | A | T | L | C | M | O |

## Chapter 5

**Short Yardage Crossword (from page 58)**

Additional Clue Answer: GREER

|  | P | R | O | T | H | R | O |  |
|---|---|---|---|---|---|---|---|---|
| F | L | A | T | H | E | A | D | S |
| A | U | S | T | R | A | L | I | A |
| T | S | P |  | E | V | E | N | T |
|  |  |  | B | E | E |  |  |  |
| B | A | B | E | S |  | S | P | A |
| A | N | A | L | O | G | I | E | S |
| D | E | C | I | M | A | T | E | S |
|  | W | H | E | E | L | E | R |  |

**Who am I? Sudoku (from page 64)**

Don HUTSON

| T | H | U | N | S | O |
|---|---|---|---|---|---|
| S | O | N | H | T | U |
| H | U | T | S | O | N |
| N | S | O | T | U | H |
| O | T | H | U | N | S |
| U | N | S | O | H | T |

**Dynamic Duos (from page 64)**

2010—JONES, HANKS; 2009—MAZE, PEEK; 2008—WALKER, ALEXANDER; 2007—MCCOY, GRANT; 2006—BROWN, OAKLEY; 2005—HALL, CADDELL; 2004—PROTHO, KNIGHT; 2003—LUKE, FULGHAM.

**Building Blocks (from page 69)**

1. A; 2. LA; 3. ALE; 4. MEAL; 5. MAPLE; 6. PALMER.

## Offsides Sudoku (from page 61)

| | | | | | | | | |
|---|---|---|---|---|---|---|---|---|
| T | L | M | C | S | A | R | I | E |
| C | R | S | I | M | E | T | L | A |
| I | E | L | T | A | S | M | R | C |
| A | S | T | L | C | I | E | M | R |
| S | M | C | E | R | T | I | A | L |
| L | A | I | R | E | M | S | C | T |
| R | C | E | M | I | L | A | T | S |
| M | T | A | S | L | R | C | E | I |
| E | I | R | A | T | C | L | S | M |

## McCalister Sudoku (from page 61)

| | | | | | | | | |
|---|---|---|---|---|---|---|---|---|
| I | A | S | L | M | R | C | T | E |
| L | M | T | C | I | E | S | R | A |
| E | C | R | A | T | S | M | L | I |
| R | E | A | M | C | T | L | I | S |
| S | L | C | E | R | I | A | M | T |
| M | T | I | S | A | L | E | C | R |
| T | S | E | I | L | C | R | A | M |
| C | R | M | T | E | A | I | S | L |
| A | I | L | R | S | M | T | E | C |

## Change a Letter (from page 69)

1. GREG PAYNE; 2. HOWARD CROSS; 3. JOEY JONES; 4. TERRY JONES; 5. SAM COLLINS; 6. AL BELL; 7. JIMMY DILL; 8. BOBBY LUNA.

## Receivers Trivia (from page 66)

1. Wide receiver Prince Wimbley.
2. Jason McAddley (110 yards) and Freddie Milons (109).
3. D.J. Hall.
4. D.J. Hall vs. Tennessee.
5. David Palmer vs. Vanderbilt.
6. D.J. Hall (twice), David Palmer and Julio Jones.

7. Michael Vaughn vs. Southern Mississippi.
8. David Palmer.
9. Tyrone Prothro.
10. Tyrone Prothro.
11. Freddie Milons.
12. Mike Price at UTEP.
13. Quincy Jackson.
14. Lamonde Russell.
15. Howard Cross.
16. Patrick Hape.
17. Ozzie Newsome.
18. Ozzie Newsome.
19. Ray Perkins.
20. Dennis Homan.
21. Don Hutson.
22. David Ray with 19 catches.
23. Paul Bryant.
24. Ozzie Newsome.
25. Ray Perkins.

**Receivers Crossword (from page 62)**

| I | N | S | T | ■ | U | G | L | I | ■ | E | V | A | D | E |
|---|---|---|---|---|---|---|---|---|---|---|---|---|---|---|
| T | U | T | U | ■ | G | O | A | D | ■ | V | I | R | U | S |
| S | T | A | R | ■ | H | O | M | E | ■ | I | N | G | O | T |
| ■ | ■ | R | N | A | ■ | ■ | B | A | I | L | E | Y | ■ | ■ |
| I | N | V | E | R | T | S | ■ | L | S | D | ■ | L | E | A |
| M | E | E | R | K | A | T | S | ■ | M | O | W | E | R | S |
| P | O | D | ■ | ■ | L | I | K | E | ■ | E | A | S | E | S |
| ■ | ■ | ■ | R | E | C | E | I | V | E | R | S | ■ | ■ | ■ |
| P | E | S | O | S | ■ | S | E | E | P | ■ | ■ | M | E | W |
| S | E | N | E | C | A | ■ | D | R | E | A | M | I | E | R |
| I | R | A | ■ | A | I | L | ■ | T | E | P | I | D | L | Y |
| ■ | ■ | P | A | L | M | E | R | ■ | ■ | E | L | D | ■ | ■ |
| S | E | P | I | A | ■ | A | U | N | T | ■ | O | L | L | A |
| A | G | E | N | T | ■ | S | L | O | E | ■ | N | E | A | P |
| T | O | R | T | E | ■ | T | E | R | N | ■ | S | C | O | T |

### Receivers Word Search (from page 65)

| J | T | H | W | L | U | N | A | B | W | A | L | K | E | R |
|---|---|---|---|---|---|---|---|---|---|---|---|---|---|---|
| S | P | U | G | H | W | H | O | M | A | N | W | H | S | L |
| E | I | I | K | O | E | K | U | L | W | I | I | I | G | L |
| N | T | S | R | U | H | E | T | I | H | W | L | Q | R | E |
| O | R | B | A | F | I | L | L | N | S | L | L | E | A | B |
| J | R | D | U | M | L | Y | W | E | I | I | I | W | Y | N |
| G | E | Y | T | M | A | E | K | W | R | Y | A | R | E | P |
| P | G | E | O | P | R | O | T | H | R | O | M | W | N | E |
| A | A | S | L | P | Y | U | W | C | M | K | S | R | O | R |
| L | N | S | L | B | A | I | S | I | H | O | O | E | S | K |
| M | A | X | E | L | L | Y | L | S | M | E | N | T | K | I |
| E | R | C | S | S | I | O | N | E | E | C | R | R | C | N |
| R | K | B | O | P | N | D | P | E | A | L | N | A | A | S |
| N | D | N | N | S | N | H | G | U | A | V | L | C | J | W |
| L | L | A | H | R | I | C | H | A | R | D | S | O | N | T |

## Chapter 6

### Short Yardage Crossword (from page 70)

Additional Clue Answer: MASON

|  | A | B | A |  | A | P | O | S |
|---|---|---|---|---|---|---|---|---|
|  | M | A | R | A | D | O | N | A |
| J | E | R | U | S | A | L | E | M |
| O | R | I | B | I |  | A | L | P |
| H | I | T | A |  | A | R | I | L |
| N | C | O |  | O | N | I | N | E |
| S | A | N | I | T | I | Z | E | S |
| O | N | E | M | E | T | E | R |  |
| N | A | S | A |  | A | S | S |  |

### Howard Sudoku (from page 73)

| W | O | R | D | A | H |
|---|---|---|---|---|---|
| A | D | H | O | W | R |
| H | A | O | R | D | W |
| D | R | W | H | O | A |
| O | H | A | W | R | D |
| R | W | D | A | H | O |

## O-Line Name Grid (from page 74)

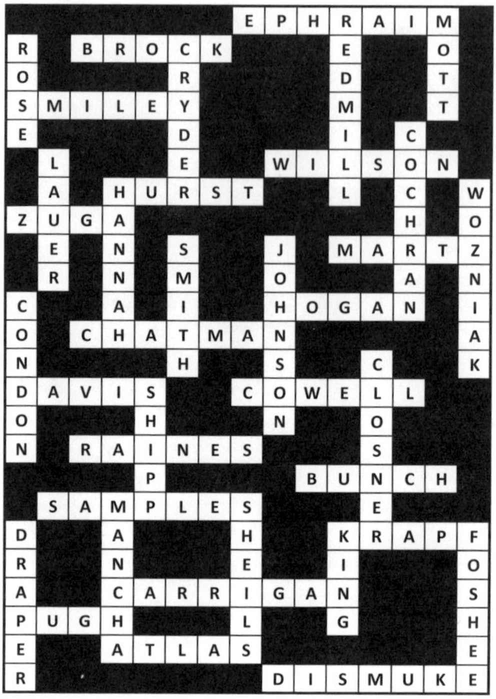


## Offensive Line Word Search (from page 82)

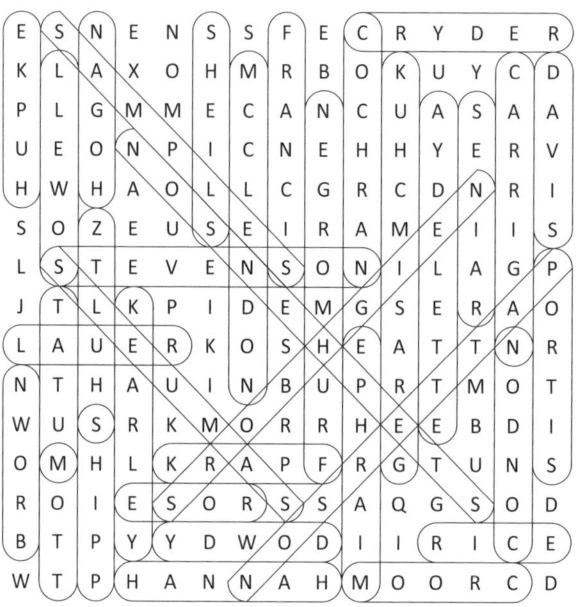

**J.B. Closner Sudoku (from page 73)**

| S | O | E | B | N | L | R | J | C |
|---|---|---|---|---|---|---|---|---|
| B | L | C | R | J | O | N | S | E |
| R | N | J | S | E | C | B | O | L |
| E | R | O | J | C | S | L | N | B |
| N | B | C | L | O | E | S | R | J |
| J | L | S | N | B | R | C | E | O |
| C | J | R | O | S | B | E | L | N |
| L | E | N | C | R | J | O | B | S |
| O | S | B | E | L | N | J | C | R |

**Offensive Line Crossword (from page 76)**

| P | A | C | E |  | O | B | E | S | E |  | M | O | L | D |
|---|---|---|---|---|---|---|---|---|---|---|---|---|---|---|
| O | L | D | S |  | C | A | P | E | R |  | A | R | I | A |
| S | O | R | T |  | C | R | E | T | E |  | T | E | A | R |
| T | H | O |  | T | U | B | E |  | C | O | H | O | R | T |
| S | A | M | U | E | L | S |  | E | T | U | I |  |  |  |
|  |  |  | S | A | T |  | S | C | O | T | S | M | E | N |
| L | A | C | E | S |  | P | O | O | R |  |  | A | L | A |
| E | R | O | D | E |  | A | L | L |  | S | A | L | S | A |
| A | G | A |  |  | V | I | I | I |  | O | F | T | E | N |
| F | O | X | H | O | U | N | D |  | S | P | A |  |  |  |
|  |  |  | A | W | L | S |  | E | P | H | R | A | I | M |
| B | O | N | N | E | T |  | I | R | I | S |  | F | D | A |
| U | P | O | N |  | U | N | B | A | R |  | L | I | E | U |
| L | A | V | A |  | R | A | I | S | E |  | O | R | A | L |
| B | L | A | H |  | E | N | D | E | D |  | G | E | L | S |

**Fill the Grid (from page 83)**

| R | E | D |
|---|---|---|
| O | A | R |
| T | R | Y |

| S | T | A | G |
|---|---|---|---|
| H | I | L | L |
| E | D | G | E |
| D | E | A | N |

### Offensive Line Trivia (from page 78)

1. Andre Smith.
2. New England Patriots.
3. Tampa Bay Buccaneers (1977-82) and Los Angeles Raiders (1983-88).
4. Cecil Dowdy, Jr.
5. Cecil Dowdy, Jr.
6. Atlanta Falcons in the third round.
7. Andre Smith at Birmingham Huffman HS.
8. Antoine Caldwell.
9. Chris Samuels.
10. Sylvester Croom.
11. Leroy Monsky.
12. Bill Lee.
13. James Carpenter, D.J. Fluker, Barrett Jones, Alfred McCullough, Anthony Steen, William Vlachos and Chance Warmack.
14. Chance Warmack.
15. Joey Jones.
16. Barrett Jones.
17. Barrett Jones.
18. D.J. Fluker.
19. Alfred McCullough.
20. Jeff Stoutland.
21. James Carpenter.
22. Guard George Wilson.
23. Dwight Stephenson.
24. Wes Neighbors and Larry Rose.
25. Center Paul Crane, who played for UA in 1963-65, earning All-America honors.

## Chapter 7

### Short Yardage Crossword (from page 84)

Additional Clue Answer: CURRY

| | | | | | | | | |
|---|---|---|---|---|---|---|---|---|
| H | A | L | L | ■ | C | O | D | Y |
| U | V | E | A | ■ | O | D | E | A |
| E | E | N | Y | ■ | W | I | S | P |
| D | O | T | S | T | H | E | I | S |
| ■ | ■ | ■ | A | C | E | ■ | ■ | ■ |
| E | V | E | N | B | R | E | A | K |
| R | I | L | E | ■ | D | C | C | I |
| I | D | I | G | ■ | E | R | I | N |
| K | I | N | G | ■ | R | U | D | D |

### Baumhower Sudoku (from page 87)

| | | | | | | | | |
|---|---|---|---|---|---|---|---|---|
| B | U | O | M | A | H | W | R | E |
| A | M | R | O | W | E | U | B | H |
| E | W | H | B | R | U | A | O | M |
| W | R | E | H | O | M | B | A | U |
| U | H | B | A | E | W | O | M | R |
| O | A | M | U | B | R | H | E | W |
| R | O | U | E | H | A | M | W | B |
| H | E | A | W | M | B | R | U | O |
| M | B | W | R | U | O | E | H | A |

## Defensive Players Crossword (from page 88)

| | | | | | | | | | | | | | | |
|---|---|---|---|---|---|---|---|---|---|---|---|---|---|---|
| U | S | E | D | ■ | J | O | L | T | S | ■ | ■ | S | P | A |
| G | O | N | E | ■ | O | C | E | A | N | ■ | W | O | R | N |
| L | O | D | E | ■ | R | H | I | N | O | ■ | R | U | I | N |
| I | N | S | P | A | D | E | S | ■ | W | H | E | N | C | E |
| ■ | ■ | ■ | ■ | P | A | R | ■ | S | P | A | N | D | E | X |
| U | N | S | E | E | N | ■ | M | Y | E | R | S | ■ | ■ | ■ |
| S | O | I | L | ■ | ■ | A | U | R | A | S | ■ | A | N | A |
| S | N | A | F | U | ■ | G | N | U | ■ | H | U | M | O | R |
| R | E | M | ■ | N | A | A | C | P | ■ | ■ | S | P | A | M |
| ■ | ■ | ■ | S | M | I | T | H | ■ | T | R | A | S | H | Y |
| U | N | A | W | A | R | E | ■ | W | H | O | ■ | ■ | ■ | ■ |
| R | U | N | I | N | S | ■ | R | H | O | M | B | O | I | D |
| G | R | I | N | ■ | I | D | I | O | M | ■ | O | B | O | E |
| E | S | S | E | ■ | C | O | C | O | A | ■ | S | I | T | E |
| S | E | E | ■ | ■ | K | E | E | P | S | ■ | S | T | A | R |

## Defensive Players Word Search (from page 91)

| | | | | | | | | | | | | | | |
|---|---|---|---|---|---|---|---|---|---|---|---|---|---|---|
| T | N | O | C | A | B | O | D | Q | B | M | B | J | H | P |
| H | C | L | A | R | K | F | A | N | L | L | R | F | B | I |
| O | Y | S | E | L | Y | L | R | N | A | O | O | N | R | T |
| M | K | R | A | U | S | S | E | E | I | H | W | O | A | T |
| A | G | W | R | T | R | C | W | P | R | F | N | S | G | S |
| S | R | M | S | U | N | Z | O | O | S | I | F | N | G | T |
| R | O | C | I | I | C | I | H | P | N | E | H | I | S | E |
| E | I | N | T | A | R | S | M | I | E | A | N | B | R | A |
| C | N | E | U | V | R | R | U | Z | L | L | N | O | Q | G |
| N | U | A | D | E | M | R | A | L | O | O | A | R | J | U |
| E | J | L | T | U | E | J | B | H | T | N | P | N | S | E |
| P | R | L | G | K | K | D | X | R | X | D | D | I | D | P |
| S | A | N | R | D | O | E | U | S | N | O | Y | L | R | V |
| W | A | A | P | N | U | B | S | H | E | N | I | L | C | T |
| M | P | P | S | I | V | R | A | J | N | O | S | L | E | N |

**LOWE Combos (from page 90)**

ELOW, LEWO, WLEO.

**Build the Name (from page 90)**

1. CASTILLE; 2. MITCHELL; 3. DONNELLY; 4. GILBERRY; 5. COPELAND; 6. THOMPSON; 7. JEFFRIES; 8. MILLINER; 9. SAUNDERS; 10. CONSTANT.

**Defensive Players Trivia (from page 92)**

1. Defensive lineman John Mitchell in 1971.
2. Mike DuBose.
3. Jeremiah Castille.
4. Lee Roy Jordan and Cornelius Bennett.
5. Derrick Oden.
6. Derrick Thomas.
7. Mark Barron.
8. Terrence Cody.
9. Rashad Johnson.
10. DeMeco Ryans.
11. Dwayne Rudd and Deshea Townsend.
12. Antonio Langham.
13. Eric Curry and John Copeland.
14. Keith McCants.
15. Tommy Wilcox.
16. Leroy Cook.
17. Woodrow Lowe, 134 in 1973.
18. Antonio Langham, 19 from 1990-93.
19. Hootie Ingram, 10 in 1952.
20. DeMeco Ryans, 25 vs. Arkansas in 2003.
21. Wayne Davis, 327 from 1983-86.
22. Derrick Thomas, 52 from 1985-88, more than twice as many as the second highest total.
23. Ester James.
24. Marty Lyons.
25. Mike Riley.

**What is It? (from page 95)**

1. GOAL LINE STAND; 2. DOUBLE COVERAGE; 3. BUMP AND RUN; 4. INCOMPLETE PASS; 5. MIDDLE GUARD; 6. CORNERBACK; 7. TOO MANY MEN ON THE FIELD.

# Chapter 8

### Short Yardage Crossword
### (from page 96)

Additional Clue Answer: THOMAS

| A | S | H | Y | | | G | S | A |
|---|---|---|---|---|---|---|---|---|
| C | L | U | E | | H | O | L | T |
| H | U | R | T | | O | G | E | E |
| E | R | R | | A | B | E | D | |
| | | I | F | N | O | T | | |
| | A | C | I | D | | T | H | O |
| E | L | A | N | | T | E | E | N |
| M | A | N | N | | O | R | A | L |
| U | S | E | | | E | S | P | Y |

### Gilmer Sudoku
### (from page 99)

| I | E | M | R | G | L |
|---|---|---|---|---|---|
| G | R | L | E | M | I |
| M | I | E | L | R | G |
| L | G | R | I | E | M |
| E | M | I | G | L | R |
| R | L | G | M | I | E |

### Special Teams Trivia (from page 102)

1. Ryan Pflugner.
2. Number 90.
3. Cade Foster.
4. True.
5. Trent Richardson.
6. Marquis Maze.
7. Philip Doyle.
8. Jamie Christensen.
9. Van Tiffin.
10. Seven.
11. Neal Thomas.
12. Philip Doyle.
13. Philip Doyle.
14. Leigh Tiffin.
15. Leigh Tiffin.
16. Tennessee, 9-6.
17. Ryan Pflugner.
18. Thomas Rayam.
19. 19 punts.
20. Greg Gantt.
21. Daniel Pope.
22. 89 yards.
23. Tyrone Prothro.
24. Brandon Brooks.
25. Chris James.

## Special Teams Crossword (from page 100)

| | | | | | | | | | | | | | | |
|---|---|---|---|---|---|---|---|---|---|---|---|---|---|---|
| M | O | H | R | | S | P | R | Y | | B | A | T | E | D |
| E | P | E | E | | T | R | U | E | | O | L | I | V | E |
| N | A | R | C | | R | E | F | S | | S | I | N | E | W |
| S | L | O | E | | O | F | F | | S | T | A | Y | S | |
| | | | N | A | P | A | | L | E | I | S | | | |
| G | A | N | T | T | | B | L | A | N | C | | S | P | A |
| A | G | I | L | E | | | A | M | O | K | | H | A | N |
| L | A | C | Y | | W | A | D | E | R | | B | O | N | G |
| E | T | H | | P | E | R | E | | | D | O | W | E | L |
| S | E | E | | R | E | I | N | S | | D | O | Y | L | E |
| | | | B | O | N | D | | W | A | T | T | | | |
| | M | E | R | C | Y | | V | I | P | | C | O | S | T |
| L | I | M | I | T | | D | I | V | A | | A | R | T | Y |
| A | M | I | N | O | | A | V | E | R | | M | E | E | K |
| P | E | T | E | R | | M | A | L | T | | P | O | P | E |

## Special Teams Word Search (from page 105)

| | | | | | | | | | | | | | | |
|---|---|---|---|---|---|---|---|---|---|---|---|---|---|---|
| E | R | S | A | M | N | E | D | R | A | E | B | A | W | E |
| G | E | A | N | O | S | M | A | I | L | L | I | W | Y | M |
| I | M | N | T | Y | S | T | O | C | K | T | O | N | O | K |
| L | L | E | W | O | H | W | T | H | Z | T | A | H | C | S |
| M | A | R | E | R | M | E | F | A | L | N | R | U | V | H |
| E | P | A | L | L | O | S | V | R | H | A | N | M | N | E |
| R | R | K | Y | E | F | T | D | D | E | G | O | P | E | L |
| P | A | N | O | C | M | R | C | S | I | E | S | H | L | B |
| T | N | I | D | M | A | K | E | O | D | P | L | R | S | Y |
| R | A | F | Q | H | N | C | U | N | R | O | I | E | O | U |
| L | G | F | C | M | N | I | L | Y | G | P | W | Y | N | E |
| I | E | I | O | R | H | T | O | R | P | U | X | P | M | D |
| D | R | T | Y | A | E | S | M | A | I | L | L | I | W | O |
| I | Z | O | A | S | N | O | M | M | I | S | K | F | I | O |
| F | T | N | A | Y | R | B | B | S | U | T | T | E | P | G |

**Pflugner Sudoku (from page 99)**

| | | | | | | | |
|---|---|---|---|---|---|---|---|
| U | L | R | N | E | F | P | G |
| E | F | G | P | R | U | L | N |
| R | E | U | L | F | N | G | P |
| F | N | P | G | U | L | R | E |
| P | U | L | E | G | R | N | F |
| G | R | N | F | P | E | U | L |
| L | P | E | U | N | G | F | R |
| N | G | F | R | L | P | E | U |

## Chapter 9

**Short Yardage Crossword (from page 106)**

Additional Clue Answer: SCOTT

| | | | | | | | | |
|---|---|---|---|---|---|---|---|---|
| ■ | I | M | P | ■ | A | P | E | ■ |
| ■ | D | O | E | ■ | D | E | N | ■ |
| ■ | E | R | A | ■ | O | N | E | ■ |
| I | N | T | R | O | ■ | I | R | A |
| S | T | A | L | L | I | N | G | S |
| M | I | L | ■ | D | O | S | E | S |
| ■ | C | I | G | ■ | T | U | T | ■ |
| ■ | A | T | E | ■ | A | L | I | ■ |
| ■ | L | Y | E | ■ | S | A | C | ■ |

**Thomas Sudoku (from page 116)**

| | | | | | |
|---|---|---|---|---|---|
| T | S | A | O | M | H |
| M | H | O | T | S | A |
| S | T | H | A | O | M |
| O | A | M | H | T | S |
| A | M | T | S | H | O |
| H | O | S | M | A | T |

**Cryptic Quote (from page 110)**

"LITTLE THINGS MAKE THE DIFFERENCE. EVERYONE IS WELL PREPARED IN THE BIG THINGS, BUT ONLY THE WINNERS PERFECT THE LITTLE THINGS."

**Who am I? Sudoku (from page 116)**

GUY LOWMAN

| | | | | | | | | | |
|---|---|---|---|---|---|---|---|---|---|
| ► | G | U | Y | L | O | W | M | A | N |
| | N | O | W | G | M | A | L | Y | U |
| | M | A | L | Y | N | U | O | G | W |
| | A | Y | G | M | W | L | U | N | O |
| | L | N | U | O | Y | G | A | W | M |
| | O | W | M | U | A | N | G | L | Y |
| | W | L | A | N | U | M | Y | O | G |
| | U | G | O | W | L | Y | N | M | A |
| | Y | M | N | A | G | O | W | U | L |

**Nick Saban Wordsmith Challenge (from page 109)**

ABACI, ABACK, ABAS, AINS, AKIN, ANAS, ANIS, ANNA, ANNAS, ANSA, ASCI, BAAS, BACK, BACKS, BANI, BANIAN, BANIANS, BANK, BANKS, BANKSIA, BANNS, BANS, BASIC, BASIN, BASK, BIAS, BINS, BISK, CABIN, CABINS, CABS, CAIN, CAINS, CANAKIN, CANAKINS, CANNA, CANNABIS, CANNAS, CANS, CASA, CASK, INKS, INNS, ISBA, KAAS, KABS, KAIN, KAINS, KANA, KANAS, KANBAN, KANBANS, KINA, KINAS, KINS, NAAN, NAANS, NABIS, NABS, NANA, NANAS, NANS, NIBS, NICK, NICKS, SABIN, SACK, SAIN, SAKI, SANK, SCAB, SCAN, SICK, SIKA, SINK, SKIN, SNACK, SNIB, SNICK.

**Coaches Crossword (from page 114)**

| | | | | | | | | | | | | | | |
|---|---|---|---|---|---|---|---|---|---|---|---|---|---|---|
| ■ | M | O | H | A | W | K | ■ | ■ | A | S | H | E | N | ■ |
| P | A | R | A | N | O | I | A | ■ | T | H | E | S | I | S |
| O | U | T | L | I | N | E | S | ■ | T | U | S | S | L | E |
| E | L | S | E | ■ | ■ | V | I | G | I | L | ■ | E | E | N |
| ■ | ■ | ■ | S | K | I | ■ | M | O | L | A | R | ■ | ■ | ■ |
| C | R | A | T | E | D | ■ | O | V | A | ■ | N | O | E | S |
| H | E | W | ■ | L | E | A | V | E | ■ | S | A | B | A | N |
| E | R | A | ■ | L | A | P | ■ | R | O | C | ■ | E | G | O |
| C | U | R | R | Y | ■ | L | I | N | G | O | ■ | S | E | W |
| K | N | E | E | ■ | M | O | M | ■ | E | T | H | E | R | S |
| ■ | ■ | ■ | S | K | I | M | P | ■ | E | T | A | ■ | ■ | ■ |
| E | M | U | ■ | I | M | B | U | E | ■ | ■ | R | A | T | A |
| L | A | T | I | N | O | ■ | R | A | T | H | O | L | E | S |
| F | L | A | R | E | S | ■ | E | C | H | E | L | O | N | S |
| ■ | L | H | A | S | A | ■ | ■ | H | E | R | D | E | D | ■ |

### Coaches Trivia (from page 111)

1. Ron Middleton.
2. Illinois, 21-15.
3. True, but he never played pro football.
4. Maryland in 1945.
5. A gold ring inscribed "The Junction Boys" in honor of his 1954 Texas A&M team.
6. Presidential Medal of Freedom, the nation's highest civilian award.
7. *Sport Illustrated.*
8. Joe Kines.
9. False, he's the son of the NFL's all-time winningest coach.
10. John Mitchell in 1973, just a year after graduating from UA.
11. Texas State University-San Marcos.
12. Texas Christian.
13. Mike DuBose.
14. Ray Perkins.
15. Gene Stallings.
16. Bill Curry.
17. Jennings Whitworth, who was 4-24-2 in three seasons.
18. Frank Thomas.
19. Wallace Wade.
20. Mike Price.

### Nick Saban Trivia (from page 113)

1. Bear Bryant, at Alabama and Kentucky.
2. Houston Oilers (1988-89), Cleveland Browns (1991-94) and Miami Dolphins (2005-06).
3. Toledo.
4. Oklahoma, 21-14.
5. *The Blind Side.*

## Chapter 10

### Missing B-A-M-A (from page 121)

1. BARMAID; 2. ARMBAND; 3. MACABRE; 4. LAMBAST; 5. BANTAMS; 6. BATHMAT; 7. AMIABLE; 8. BOATMAN; 9. MAILBAG; 10. ABYSMAL.

### Tide TXT (from page 126)

1. BARKER; 2. JOHNSON; 3. THOMAS; 4. INGRAM; 5. RYANS; 6. PROCTOR; 7. BENNETT; 8. MCCLAIN.

### Across and Down Words (from page 127)

Across: RUSH, PASS, PLAY, PUNT, BALL, FLAG, ENDS; Down: TACKLED, QUARTER, DEFENSE, KICKOFF; Phrase: SOUTHEASTERN CONFERENCE CHAMPS.

**Short Yardage Crossword (from page 118)**

Additional Clue Answer: NABORS

| | | | | | | | | |
|---|---|---|---|---|---|---|---|---|
| | R | U | S | S | I | A | N | |
| | O | R | L | A | N | D | O | |
| | A | G | E | N | D | A | S | |
| | N | E | W | S | O | M | E | |
| | | | | | | | | |
| B | O | Y | D | | C | A | I | N |
| L | O | A | D | | Y | O | R | E |
| E | Z | R | A | | S | N | O | W |
| D | E | N | Y | | T | E | N | T |

**Nesbit Sudoku (from page 131)**

| | | | | | |
|---|---|---|---|---|---|
| N | B | S | T | E | I |
| E | I | T | N | B | S |
| S | N | B | E | I | T |
| I | T | E | S | N | B |
| B | S | N | I | T | E |
| T | E | I | B | S | N |

**Find the Words (from page 125)**

ABODE, ABOIL, ABOLLA, ABOMA, ABORT, ABRI,ALAMO, ALAMODE, ALAMORT, ALAR, ALDOL, ALIT,ALLEL, ALLOBAR, ALLOD, ALLOT, ALMA, ALOD, AMLA, AMOLE, AMORAL, AMORT, ARID, ARIL,ARILED, ARIOT, AROID, AROLLA, AROMA, ARTI, BALD, BALE, BALED, BALL, BALLED, BALM, BARILLA, BOAR, BOART, BODE, BODLE, BOIL, BOILED, BOLA, BOLAR, BOLD, BOLE, BOLIDE, BOLL, BOLLED, BOMA, BORA, BORAL, BORIDE, BORT, BRIDE, BRIDLE, BRILL, BRIO, BRIT, BROD, BROIL, BROILED, BROMAL, DELI, DELO, DILL, DIOL, DIORAMA, DIRAM, DIRT, DOAB, DOBRA, DOIT, DOLE, DOLL, DOLMA, DOMAL, DORB, DORBA, DORT, EDIT, EDITOR, IDLE, IDOL, IDOLA, LABOR, LABRID, LABROID, LAMA, LARI, LAROID, LIDO, LILL, LILLED, LILO, LIRA, LIROT, LITORAL, LLAMA, LOAM, LOBAR, LODE, LOID, LOIR, LOMA, LORIOT, LOTI, LOTO, MALA, MALAR, MALE, MALI, MALL, MALLED, MALODOR, MALOTI, MARID, MART, MODE, MODEL, MODELLI, MODELLO, MODI, MOIL, MOILED, MOIRA, MOIT, MOLA, MOLAL, MOLAR, MOLD, MOLE, MOLL, MOLLA, MORA, MORAL, MORALE, MORALL, MORALLED, MORT, MOTI, MOTILE, MOTOR, ODOR, OILED, OLID, OLIO, OLLA, ORAL, ORIOLE, RALE, RAMAL, RIDE, RILE, RILED, RILL, RILLE, RILLED, RIOT, ROAM, RODE, ROIL, ROILED, ROLE, ROLL, ROLLED, ROMA, ROMAL, ROTI, ROTO, ROTOR, TIDE, TILDE, TILE, TILED, TILL, TILLED, TIRO, TOIL, TOILE, TOILED, TOLA, TOLAR, TOLD, TOLE, TOLED, TOLEDO, TOLL, TOLLED, TORA, TORI, TRAM, TRIDE, TRILD, TRILL, TRILLED, TRIO, TRIODE, TRIOL, TRIOR, TROD, TRODE, TROLL, TROLLED.

**Roll Tide Categories (from page 128)**

Offensive Players: RUTLEDGE, OGILVIE, LEWIS, LUKE, TURNER, INGRAM, DOWDY, EPHRAIM; Defensive Players: RYANS, ODEN, LANGHAM, LYONS, THOMAS, IVY, DIXON, EDWARDS; Football Terms: RUNNING BACK, OFFSIDES, LINEMAN, LINEBACKER, TACKLE, INTERCEPTION, DEFENSE, EXTRA POINT; Alabama Cities: RUSSELLVILLE, OXFORD, LEEDS, LINCOLN, TUSCALOOSA, IRONDALE, DOTHAN, ENTERPRISE.

## Overtime Crossword (from page 122)

| | | | | | | | | | | | | | | |
|---|---|---|---|---|---|---|---|---|---|---|---|---|---|---|
| C | G | I | ■ | U | P | D | A | T | E | ■ | S | P | R | Y |
| L | A | M | ■ | S | E | E | S | A | W | ■ | H | O | P | E |
| O | R | B | ■ | I | N | C | I | T | E | D | O | R | M | S |
| U | N | I | O | N | ■ | O | F | T | ■ | Y | E | T | ■ | ■ |
| D | E | B | U | G | ■ | ■ | ■ | O | R | E | ■ | E | A | T |
| S | T | E | T | ■ | C | O | C | O | A | ■ | O | N | T | O |
| ■ | ■ | ■ | B | O | R | E | R | ■ | K | I | T | T | E | N |
| ■ | ■ | M | I | N | O | R | E | D | I | C | T | S | ■ | ■ |
| S | H | A | D | O | W | ■ | P | A | S | E | O | ■ | ■ | ■ |
| A | R | C | S | ■ | D | O | E | T | H | ■ | M | O | D | E |
| C | S | A | ■ | P | S | I | ■ | ■ | ■ | M | A | R | R | Y |
| ■ | ■ | R | I | O | ■ | L | E | A | ■ | I | N | D | I | E |
| E | R | O | T | I | C | M | I | N | D | S | ■ | E | L | L |
| M | A | N | E | ■ | P | A | R | T | E | D | ■ | A | L | I |
| S | W | I | M | ■ | U | N | E | S | C | O | ■ | L | S | D |

## One and Only One (from page 124)

| | | | | | | | | | | | | | | |
|---|---|---|---|---|---|---|---|---|---|---|---|---|---|---|
| N | K | I | E | I | N | N | K | E | I | N | I | K | I | N |
| I | K | E | N | K | I | E | N | I | K | K | I | N | E | I |
| K | E | I | N | I | E | K | I | I | K | N | I | K | N | K |
| N | I | K | K | E | I | N | K | K | E | N | E | K | N | I |
| N | I | K | K | N | N | I | K | I | N | K | I | N | K | E |
| I | K | E | N | I | K | I | K | E | N | I | K | K | E | I |
| N | K | I | E | E | E | K | K | K | I | I | I | **N** | N | N |
| I | N | K | E | N | K | K | I | I | N | I | **I** | K | I | I |
| K | I | I | N | K | E | N | K | I | E | **K** | N | E | K | N |
| I | N | K | E | K | I | K | E | E | **E** | K | I | E | I | E |
| N | E | K | E | K | K | I | E | E | N | K | I | I | K | N |
| I | E | K | K | E | N | N | E | I | I | K | E | K | I | K |
| K | N | I | N | N | E | N | N | E | N | I | N | I | E | I |
| N | E | K | I | I | N | K | E | I | N | N | K | E | N | I |
| I | N | I | E | I | K | E | I | K | E | I | N | K | I | N |

### Overtime Trivia (from page 129)

1. Gene Stallings.
2. Joe Sewell.
3. Johnny Mack Brown.
4. 11 game winning streak. (Tennessee's longest winning streak is seven games.)
5. Foy-ODK Sportsmanship Award.
6. Million Dollar Band.
7. Mike Slive.
8. Forrest Gump.
9. Gary Busey.
10. Rodney Clark.
11. Ken Stabler.
12. Joe Namath.
13. Houndstooth, in honor of Bear Bryant.
14. George H. Denny was named president of UA in 1912, a post he held for nearly a quarter of a century.
15. 1929.
16. Florida in 1963 and Southern Mississippi in 1982.
17. It was UA's first night game.
18. It was UA's first televised game.
19. Notre Dame is 5-1 against Bama and Texas is 7-1-1.
20. Howard, but the two teams haven't played since 1944.
21. It is the pledge made at convocation by each incoming freshman class.
22. Dr. Robert E. Witt.
23. Denny.
24. Eli Gold.
25. Jimmy Carter.

## Praise for *Prompting Deeper Discussions*

"Matthew Kay reminds us that vibrant student talk is the heartbeat of any engaging classroom, and *Prompting Deeper Discussions* provides teachers with in-depth practical steps for starting—and extending—deeper student conversations. As James Britton famously said, 'Reading and writing float on a sea of talk,' and this book is a valuable resource for centering this important talk in your classroom."

—**Kelly Gallagher**, author of *Readicide: How Our Schools Are Killing Reading and What You Can Do About It*

"In *Prompting Deeper Discussions,* teacher Matt Kay pulls back the curtain on crafting questions that lead to fabulous classroom conversations. Through his clear analysis, illuminating classroom examples, and lively writing, Kay shares his classroom-tested approaches with fellow educators, equipping us to adapt his simple, powerful planning and implementation techniques for our specific teaching contexts. Prompting and facilitating deep, engaging, productive discussions isn't magic, and it's no longer mystery, thanks to Kay's superb, tight, useful book. Highly recommended!"

—**Tracy Johnston Zager**, author of *Becoming the Math Teacher You Wish You'd Had: Ideas and Strategies from Vibrant Classrooms*

"Clearly and concisely, Matthew Kay delivers the essential pedagogical moves necessary to lead and deepen classroom discussion. *Prompting Deeper Discussions* will help new and experienced teachers alike how to think more intentionally about how they structure their discussions and anticipate and handle the dilemmas and issues teachers often face in this important aspect of instruction. Drawing from his many years in the classroom, Kay has gifted us with a book for educators to meaningfully improve professional practice across the content areas."

—**Bruce Lesh**, author of *Why Won't You Just Tell Me the Answer?* and *Developing Historical Thinkers*

"A meaningful classroom discussion is perhaps the most authentic thing we can do as educators, but it also can be one of the most difficult things to structure well. What Matt has done with this book is create the conditions by which teachers can improve their facility at the classroom discussion, and make classrooms more meaningful and powerful for all their students. *Prompting Deeper Discussions* is a practitioner's book—it is written by a master teacher for teachers everywhere."

—**Chris Lehmann**, founding principal,
Science Leadership Academy

"Matthew Kay has managed another brilliant work for educators with *Prompting Deeper Discussions.* As he has done so well before, Matt opens the door to his classroom and welcomes you in to observe his planning and lessons. This book is absolutely on target for the moment we are in, and Matt connects all the dots to help readers understand the importance of class discussions and how they are facilitated. He makes the process of planning for these conversations look obvious and easy, and he gives us the tools to actually make it so!"

—**Jennifer Orr**, elementary educator and
author of *Demystifying Discussion*